Aesthetics of the Virtual

SUNY series in Contemporary Italian Philosophy
Silvia Benso and Brian Schroeder, editors

Aesthetics *of the* Virtual

ROBERTO DIODATO

Translated by Justin L. Harmon
Revised and Edited by Silvia Benso
Foreword by John Protevi

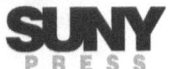

Published by State University of New York Press, Albany

© Estetica del virtuale by Roberto Diodato (Milan: Bruno Mondadori, 2005)
© 2012 State University of New York

All rights reserved

Printed in the United States of America

No part of this book may be used or reproduced in any manner whatsoever without written permission. No part of this book may be stored in a retrieval system or transmitted in any form or by any means including electronic, electrostatic, magnetic tape, mechanical, photocopying, recording, or otherwise without the prior permission in writing of the publisher.

For information, contact State University of New York Press, Albany, NY
www.sunypress.edu

Production, Laurie Searl
Marketing, Anne M. Valentine

Library of Congress Cataloging-in-Publication Data

[Estetica del virtuale. English]
  Aesthetics of the Virtual / Roberto Diodato ; Revised and Edited by Silvia Benso ; Translated by Justin L. Harmon ; Foreword by John Protevi.
       pages cm — (SUNY series in contemporary Italian philosophy)
  Includes bibliographical references and index.
  ISBN 978-1-4384-4436-9 (paperback : alk. paper)
  ISBN 978-1-4384-4435-2 (hardcover : alk. paper) 1. Virtual reality—Philosophy. 2. Art and technology. 3. Virtual reality in art. I. Benso, Silvia. II. Title.
  BD331.D5613 2012
  776—dc23
                                              2011052052

10 9 8 7 6 5 4 3 2 1

Contents

Foreword by John Protevi   *vii*

Introduction   *ix*

1. Aesthetics of the Virtual Body   *1*
2. *My* Body in the Virtual Environment   *15*
3. Forms of Expression   *35*
4. Toward the Image   *53*
5. Metaphors of the Virtual   *69*
6. The Concept of the Virtual   *91*
7. The Virtual Actor-Spectator   *101*
8. For an Aesthetics of the Hypertext   *111*

Notes   *119*

Bibliography   *147*

Index   *157*

Foreword

We philosophers have a number of animal self-images, almost a bestiary of who we are and what we do. It is as if the images of the human were too limited for what we have accepted as our calling. Thus, one of the great challenges and privileges of philosophy is to take up again the gadfly's task and to ask questions of the everyday. It is not that Socrates did not have to deal with a changing Athens, but questions of pace and tempo of change are of the utmost importance today in contemporary philosophical practice. So for us, it is not just innovations on ancient practices that need questioning; we must also attend to the questionability of what was once not so long ago a novelty but has passed too quickly into the mundane taken-for-granted. It is as if the owl of Minerva—to call upon another of our self-images—were to fly at a technological dusk that has fallen too quickly.

It is fitting that we call upon some of these self-images in introducing Roberto Diodato's *Aesthetics of the Virtual,* for the production of the self-image is at the heart of his endeavor. For a number of years we have lived with virtual reality, the ability to produce and to inhabit a computer-generated environment of images, including, with the avatar, the image of one's own body. How are such image-bodies generated, and once produced, what does it mean to inhabit such a body in such a reality? What are we seeing when we see not only images, but the image of ourselves, and not only that image, but that image seeing and interacting with all the other images of that realm?

The philosophical content of the book, one might say, is as old as our tradition and as new as could be. What are perception, imagination, representation, and many other traditional philosophical categories when applied to the realm of the virtual image? And perhaps most importantly and most strangely of all, what are we feeling when we feel these images interact, when we feel our avatar interact with other images? How is it even possible to feel something in these instances? What is virtual affect? Or, how does virtual affect come about?

Roberto Diodato's incisive book takes us on a tour of these themes, probing the fundamental human experiences of illusion, dreams, imitation, and presence. It could even be said that Diodato is interrogating the possibility of a theory of seeing in the virtual realm. Now, if theory is that which is oriented to the sight of the truth, we have to ask what does "theory" mean when our philosophical vision, our veridical vision, is aimed at the truth of the realm of virtual reality? How do we see the truth of illusion, when that illusion aims to pass itself off as reality?

The ultimate stakes of Diodato's work are thus, I believe, reflexive. What is philosophical practice when it considers the virtual? What becomes of the gadfly, the owl, and other philosophical avatars when they are turned back to consider the everyday avatars of the digital world? Densely referenced to contemporary and classical works, *Aesthetics of the Virtual* will serve for some as an introduction to these issues and for others as a challenging treatment of the phenomenological and ontological complexities found therein.

JOHN PROTEVI

Introduction

Darkness fell in from every side, a sphere of singling black, pressure on the extended crystal nerves of the universe of data he had nearly become . . .

And when he was nothing, compressed at the heart of all that dark, there came a point where the dark could be no *more*, and something tore.

The Kuang program spurted from tarnished cloud, Case's consciousness divided like beads of mercury, arcing above an endless beach the color of the dark silver clouds. His vision was spherical, as though a single retina lined the inner surface of a globe that contained all things, if all things could be counted.

And here things could be counted, each one. He knew the number of grains of sand in the construct of the beach (a number coded in a mathematical system that existed nowhere outside the mind that was Neuromancer). He knew the number of yellow food packets in the canisters in the bunker (four hundred and seven). He knew the number of brass teeth in the left half of the open zipper of the salt-crusted leather jacket that Linda Lee wore as she trudged along the sunset beach, swinging a stick of driftwood in her hand (two hundred and two).

"But you do not know her thoughts," the boy said, beside him now in the shark thing's heart. "I do not know her thoughts. You were wrong, Case. To live here is to live. There is no difference."

Many will have recognized this page from William Gibson's *Neuromancer*. In it is described an experience of virtual reality, an immersion into a world of numbers that appears in forms, images, and sensations. It is a possible experience: not actual, but possible, as it was possible to travel by submarine during Verne's time.[1] If it is a possible experience, however, and it will perhaps happen that one will live in such a world, then it is not true that there is no difference. These possible differences make up the theme of this little book. It is entitled *Aesthetics of the Virtual* because it deals with bodies that are images, with the interactions between our body—weighed down but at the same time lightened by inorganic prostheses—and those images, and with the interactions between images of our body (our *avatar*) and those image-bodies. Thus, we will look for the meaning of the conceptual constellation that rests *between* body and image, that is, perception, representation, simulacrum . . . in order to see if and how the sense of these words changes when one uses them to describe an experience of virtual environments. We will attempt to think the paradoxical notion of virtual image-body [*corpo-immagine*] and the interweaving of activity and passivity that characterizes the spectator-actor of the virtual world. We will try to distinguish the experience of the virtual from dream experience, to stabilize the difference between the virtual and the possible, and to express the particular potentiality that marks the virtual. All of this will lead to a thinking of the structure of the virtual world as essentially relational, or if one prefers, as a place that exists only in an encounter.

I have always been struck by an assertion by Robert Delaunay (quoted by Merleau-Ponty in "Eye and Mind"): "I am in Petersburg in my bed. In Paris my eyes see the sun."[2] To me, this seems simply true and also a profound opening. Virtual worlds, if I had to condense the meaning of the present work, have do with this truth.

1

Aesthetics of the Virtual Body

By "virtual body" I mean in the first place an interactive digital image,[1] the self-phenomenalization of an algorithm in binary format arising in its interaction with a user-consumer. It is a function of writing that, in its sensible appearance, at the same time exposes and conceals the translation project through which it is constituted in its computational operations. As apparition of a grammar, such a language-image [*immagine-linguaggio*] implies a peculiar spectrality that affects the visible-invisible relation and structures the modalities of its fruition. From this point of view, the digital image—which can be multisensory—is not simply image-of; it is not only a *mimesis* of that of which it is image,[2] identifiable or not, and is therefore not essentially simulacrum.[3] Nor, in any case, is it an icon[4] or original image. On the contrary, it is a genetic-relational form that belongs to a multiple system of translation. The digital image is not, one could say, properly "image," but image-body [*corpo-immagine*], since it is made of tidy sequences of binary units, or, in other words, strings of characters that develop at various levels of a syntax that constructs the coincidence between these strings and their sensible appearances, which currently are mostly sonorous or visual but in general are perceptible.[5] Now, we know that discrete sequences translate also undulating and continuous events. Therefore, as subtle body of a noncontinuous world, as discrete world of point-data that manifest themselves as fluidities and densities and saturate perception, and as (from a computer science or formal perspective) programming language, the virtual body is certainly an electronic body and therefore an atomic aggregate (to use another metaphor). The process of digitalization renders it peculiarly light, though: as a complex made up of a sometimes remarkable amount of data transmissible with extraordinary speed (the greatest speed that is possible given physical limitations), it is open to multiple embodiments that are at the same time structurally identical and phenomenally diverse insofar as the virtual body is a hybrid entity, an image-body. Its appearance, its existence-as image, is in essence interactive. This is a delicate point we shall have to return to, but which at least for now allows us to exclude from the notion of "virtual body" those simply photo-graphic or televisual digital images that allow for a passive action not affecting the properties of their appearing and that above all, at a different level of the meaning of "virtual body," do not permit a retroactive interaction with the structure of the computer memory, that is, do not permit an incision into the matrix.[6] Obviously, the degrees of interactive operativity are numerous, and so is the sense of the notion of "virtual body." Going deeper into the matter, we will now approach the robust notion of virtual body, which is of interest here due to the novelty of its ontological status.

From a simple, comprehensive, and primary point of view, "virtual body" is, for example, any visible image-object [*oggetto-immagine*] that is actually and most commonly visible on a computer screen and that allows for an interaction that can modify it, at least in the sense of activating it, of constituting it as a specific event. In most instances, the case is that of a certain type of graphic entity that, when related to another entity of the same kind, builds an environment with which the user can interact. It would be opportune to produce a phenomenology of such image-objects, which should presumably begin with a taxonomy of sites, understood as organizers of screenshots equipped with various purposes, and thus with specific problems. We are dealing here with a broad and growing field of research in which computer graphics, multimedia programming, and aesthetics of reception might collaborate. A rather interesting object in this field is the avatar,[7] that is, the representation of a non-generic human body in a Networked Virtual Environment (NVE). The case here is that of the representation of a user and his or her behaviors, of his or her virtual alter ego. I, as a consumer of this specific environment, take shape within it and appear on the screen as a graphical representation of myself. In such an environment I act, and by means of appropriate instruments, my representation/virtual body carries out the tasks I command. What the avatar does has an impact on the virtual environment, and modifies it. Such an environment is connective; participating in it are various avatars capable of interaction.[8] Especially interesting is the study of the proxemics of avatars and, in general, the attempts to reproduce the limits of the human body in a digital representation that, because of its nature, can do, within its own environment, (almost) everything (it can see or pass through objects, immediately move from one place to another, and so forth). For example, what "sense" of space can an avatar have (or, can I have through my avatar)? The human body does not have a homogeneous or merely geometrical sense of space, established only through measurable distances. Space for us is non-homogeneous, dense, and, like time, always qualitative. For programmers, this is a problem.[9]

Still in the attempt to come closer to a hard concept of virtual reality, a second exemplification of virtual body is offered by so-called immaterial sculptures. They are not digital images visible on a computer screen, but rather space-environments that take form in interaction with users, that is, virtual robots that appear in 3-D as holographic and holophonic organisms *almost* capable of "learning" data that are supplied by users and of changing in relation to them. The possibility of interaction is given through the construction of a virtual space V, resulting from the mapping of a highly singular external space E such that, through video cameras and sensors, any physical change in E can modify the state of V. A virtual sculpture is therefore perceptible as a tridimensional form luminous and sonorous in movement, and mutating in relation to the users' gestures; it can, for example, turn itself over, change direction, and disappear.[10] Such relations of mutation become more and more complex, giving rise to a metamorphosis of the virtual sculpture, to the possibility that it assumes different perceptible forms relative not only to consumers' movements, but also to their emotional states. Conceptually, the problem of an interactive metamorphosis concerns neither the possibility of registering psychophysical mutations in users (which would depend on both the quality of the sensors and a basic reductionist hypothesis), nor even the management on the part of a computer of a data bank of morphologies connectable to them. Instead, it concerns the type of relations that are instituted between the alterations of users and the generation of visible and sonorous forms. It is possible to plan, through an outline of interfaces, a system of precise translation that gives rise to a system of variation/substitution of the sculpture-configuration. Organizing a system capable of making the forms of a work evolve in relation to the interactions of users is more difficult: there is a clear divide between a type of interaction that develops within the prefixed limits of an already given materiality, in our case a data bank of remarkable dimensions, and an interaction that can shape (sculptural metaphor) the programmed matter, causing it to evolve into new, unpredictable states. Such a clear divide opens up a space in which various mediations are possible, mediations which the development of technologies and, in particular, research in evolutionary electronics, are concerned with inspecting.[11]

We can now come even closer to an approximation of the specific notion of "virtual body" by first clarifying preliminarily the qualities of the experience of the virtual, then by defining the concept of "virtuality," and finally the concept of "virtual reality." First of all, the experience of virtual reality is multimedial and interactive,[12] where "multimediality"[13] indicates a peculiar "representational wealth of a mediated environment,"[14] thinkable in its turn as constituted out of two factors: amplitude (quantity: number of senses simultaneously involved) and profundity (quality of perceptions, or sensorial information). Interactivity designates "the users' level of participation in modifying the form and content of a mediated environment,"[15] and can itself be specified in (at least) three factors: velocity (the time that it takes every datum to be assimilated into the mediated environment); range (the number of possible actions in a given environment); control ("the ability of a system to verify its own controls within a mediated environment in a natural and predictable way").[16] There exist, therefore, varying levels of multimediality and interactivity, and the experience of virtual reality will be more *immersive* depending upon the depth of such levels. One can thus maintain with Oliver Grau that "virtual realities . . . are in essence immersive"[17] while considering at the same time, however, the paradoxicality of such an affirmation insofar as physical and mental immersiveness, which implies the suspension of disbelief, and the identification of the body with the medium do not coincide with, and indeed in certain aspects stand opposed to simulation. In other words, I claim that insofar as it is immersive, "virtual reality" should not and cannot be confused with a basically perfect simulation of reality, with a simulation that annuls similarity in identity (and therefore cancels itself as such), or with a teleologically definitive transparency of medium. Immersiveness can occur, and does occur, but as quality of an experience that cannot be confused with that which we hold to be "real." To justify this position, one can examine the same question from the genetic-constituent point of view: the generation of "virtual reality" means the generation of the possibility of the experience of an environment (characterized as "environment" by a set of "virtual bodies" that are not bodies of the environment or in the environment but coincide with it) capable of producing perceptual experiences in its users. By "generator of virtual reality" we can therefore mean a machine capable of making users have the experience of such an environment, of translating an environment into a situation. Thus, a generator of virtual reality *could be* conceivable as a generator of possible sense perceptions, and, more precisely, as a generator of sense perceptions[18] (visual, auditory, tactile, olfactive, and so on) capable of simulating an environment/situation that pre-philosophically we would define as "real," as having sufficient faithfulness [*fedeltà*].[19] In short, a generator of virtual reality would simulate that "perceptual belief" seemingly presupposed in our everyday commerce with the world. I think, however, that what we have here provided is a restrictive and, all things considered, minimally interesting definition of environment and, therefore, of the virtual body, insofar as it tends to equate virtual reality and simulated reality, and therefore considers the virtual as an aspect of simulation or of a mimetic project. I think this for the following reasons: an environment that is defined as "virtual" because of its capacity to simulate a real situation results in being faithful [*fedele*] insofar as it is capable of responding in the desired way to every possible action of a user; therefore, its faithfulness does not depend only on the experiences that the users actually have, but also on those that they *could* have.[20] Now, the valuation of the "sufficiency" of faithfulness is problematic: Is it possible to simulate a reality without variation, or to construct a "perfect illusion"? Supposing that the user has the possibility of making free choices in the sense of a freedom of indifference, the simulation is impossible because such choices are not computable. Limiting ourselves to other metaphysical hypotheses, that is, assuming for simplicity's sake that the choices are the result of a causally infinite series (where the same idea of series is reductive and inadequate), the simulation of reality will be that much more efficacious the more the processor is able both to calculate the possible actions and reactions of the user and, consequently, to preconstitute the potential interactions on the part of the virtual body-environment.[21] Therefore, the virtual environment will simulate the real environment to the extent that such calculations stretch infinitely and, consequently, to the extent that such algorithms will be phenomenalizable. From this point of view, the virtual environment is an imperfect Spinozian machine, that is, an apparatus of relations that constitute a tendential coincidence between freedom and necessity, a coincidence that would be actualized only in a causal network of infinite thickness, essentially incomputable.[22] It follows that the virtual environment tends to produce the experience of an immersion pervasive and persuasive but at the same time relatively aware of its own particular ontological status: it appears as a tendential simulation and not as a perfect reproduction. In my opinion, it is this limit, this void, and this lack that open up the artistically relevant possibilities of the virtualization of the imaginary.[23]

An obvious characteristic of the virtual body, one that distinguishes it with respect to the generation of other types of digital images, is its special kind of interactivity: the virtual body is an entity that is phenomenalized through interaction. Interactivity is in certain aspects a characteristic that the virtual body has in common with any other body, but is in other respects a peculiar condition. In order to comprehend such peculiarity, that is, in order to bring oneself closer to the ontology of the virtual, it is necessary to reflect on the concept of the virtual and on the difference between the virtual and the possible. Certainly, in fact, in a general sense "the virtual is a state of the real and not the contrary of the real. There is something virtual within the real: the essences, the forms, the hidden causes, the aims that will be realized, and so on. The virtual is the active principle, the discloser of the hidden potential of the real. It is that which is at work in the real."[24] Still more in general, the "virtual" set can be considered without a doubt part of the "real" set; in fact, we use without difficulty the expression, "virtual reality."[25] However, the concept of the virtual can be better defined by means of its difference with respect to the concept of the "possible": unlike the possible, conceivable as a constituted entity that waits to be realized, the virtual is configured as a problematic complex, a node of tendencies that imposes a process of actualization. Clearly, from this point of view, the virtual-actual process is not identical with the process of realization of the possible, if the latter is conceived of as the mere bestowal of matter upon a preexistent form, and, on these lines, as constitution of substance, however dynamic it may be. On this matter, Pierre Lévy writes: "The real, substance, the thing, *subsists* or resists. The possible harbors nonmanifest forms that remain dormant: Hidden within, these determinations *insist*. The virtual . . . is a way out, an exit: it exists. The actual, however, as the manifestation of an event, *arrives*, its fundamental operation is *occurrence*."[26]

Now, the opposition to the (albeit trivialized) notion of the possible allows us to clarify the interactive quality of the virtual. To the extent that the virtual environment develops in the interactivity of its consumers, the virtual signifies a dynamic configuration of forces that have an intrinsic tendency to actualize themselves in not entirely preconstituted forms.[27]

The virtual environment in question, with its complex of perceptible qualities (color, sound, density, tactility, and so forth), that is, the environment in which I have the feeling of being immersed, is nothing else than the actualization of the content of a digital memory, the staging of an algorithm processed in a binary system.[28] This presses the question concerning the relation between *aisthesis* and *noesis*. We find ourselves in fact confronted with the possibility of a reduction of *aisthesis* (as sense perception) to computational terms, a reduction which however implies neither the reduction of secondary qualities to primary qualities nor even the possibility of reducing the world to number.[29] Rather, it speaks of an original and reversible solidarity between *aisthesis* and *noesis* that expresses itself in an operational arc one of whose extremes is constituted by a digital description in computer memory and the other by a body endowed with technological prostheses, with nonorganic extensions of the senses. The body of the user in a virtual environment is a complex structure, a subject-object resulting from a technological project; it is a quasi-cyborg body,[30] similar to what is thought of and experimented with by some artists,[31] a body that translates itself into an eminently active spectral entity.[32] A lively debate is taking place on these matters among the theorists of the virtual,[33] for a virtual environment can be known, in a certain sense, only sensibly, through an eminently corporeal gaze,[34] but at the same time [such an environment] is, as we said, a mathematization of space, and its images are the actualization of algorithms. We are here faced with a paradoxical situation: the user's very identity, the user's very I is simultaneously disembodied and hypersensitized: in order to encounter a "subtle" body, one needs to equip oneself with a "heavy" body, that is, one needs to emphasize technologically the capacities of the organic body. In this way, in my opinion, the transparency of the medium is made opaque:

In most programs, a user experiences VR through a disembodied gaze—a floating moving "perspective"—that mimes the movement of a disembodied camera eye. This is a familiar aspect of what may be called a filmic phenomenology where the camera simulates the movement of a perspective that rarely includes a self-referential visual inspection of the body as the vehicle of that perspective.[35]

To my mind, however, precisely this heaviness of the disembodiment enables us not to reduce the perspective of the virtual vision to a subjective, cinematographic process directed by oneself, and also, once again, not to reduce immersiveness to simulation. The human body/virtual body relation does not carry out a repression of corporeality thereby giving rise to a disembodied mind-eye capable of experiencing mental products that appear as sensible only by means of technological prostheses. On the contrary, virtual environments, with their "heavy" bodies related to "subtle" bodies, basically exalt the difference and the knowledge of the difference between them and usual body-environment relations. The user is thus aware of perceiving an imaginary space; the user does not have the impression of experiencing a dematerialized reality, but rather a reality perceived as "other," different, and in a certain measure similar to a product of the imagination. The possibility of manipulating one's own perspective, of turning it into the very place of experience, is combined with the possibility of learning by means of immersion[36] up to the point of allowing, at various degrees, other users' points of view to become one's own. This entails, radically and generally, a crisis in the stability and capacities of one's own body and their redefinition through the relations between technological prostheses and virtual bodies. In perspective,[37] this provokes the conceptualization of a mutable embodiment of the self, sensitive to the evolution of technology and the language of programming: that is, a rethinking of the figure of the self as a marking of its movements, of its residual integrity as medium of its transformations, of its possible boundaries within the pathways of actions that constitute the virtual space.[38]

This presses toward a further analysis of the ontological nature of the virtual, recalling with Philippe Quéau that, "the techniques of virtual representation are essentially numerical. Unlike fundamentally analogical techniques, numerical images do not participate in the real."[39] Numerical images participate in it indirectly through the process of digitalization, which is circularly made possible by those same techniques. Therefore, virtual bodies should not be understood as representations of reality, but rather as realities that are constructed in a way essentially different from those [realities] coming out of the circular engagement of a living body with the world, a world that, thanks to the vision-perception, intersects the body and becomes gesture, namely, bodily movement, is perhaps mediated by instruments of analogical reproduction, and thereby becomes image. Virtual bodies are instead "artificial windows that grant access to an intermediary world."[40] Now, in what sense is a "body" a window, in other words, a place of passage between the interior and the exterior? Perhaps the window metaphor can function if it is not understood in too banal a fashion. The issue is not that of a passage through a window of Albertian memory, because the virtual environment is not (is not only, is not essentially) a simulated reproduction of the real. Instead, the virtual body is a window-environment [*ambiente-finestra*], a peculiar place in which the internal-external relation changes according to various parameters and thereby acquires a revealing power. I will return shortly to the issue from an ontological point of view, but for now let us take our cue from a celebrated affirmation by Kandinsky: "Every phenomenon can be experienced in two different ways. These two ways are not arbitrary, but are bound up with the phenomenon—developing out of its nature and characteristics, from two of its properties: Externally-or-inwardly."[41]

This has meaning, as we know, in the first place for our own body, but also for what appears to us as to the way in which it becomes manifest: a phenomenon can be experienced in some way at a distance, it can be perceived as other, it can be world, but the very same phenomenon can nevertheless become part of our life, can carve itself into it, can occur as its *pathos* and thus manifest its invisibility in its visibility.[42] All of this corresponds to common experiences, which are as selective as they are average: something that we perceive is recorded in both memory and affectivity, entering to constitute primary and indemonstrable interiority, and eventually returning to the light of the common world through practices of various type; the mass of perceived phenomena, at least those that are consciously perceived, is nothing else. Kandinsky, however, claims not only that a phenomenon can be experienced in two different ways, internally and externally, but also that this is possible inasmuch as external and internal are properties *of* the phenomenon, of the same *phenomenon*: because it belongs to the nature of the phenomenon to be both external and internal, the phenomenon can be experienced as either world or *pathos*. Now, I do not know if this position is sustainable in relation to what we regard as "reality" in general, but it functions well with respect to virtual bodies. In a virtual body-environment, in which space is the result of an interaction, the world happens not in the manner of a distance-taking, but rather in that of a sense-feeling [*senso-sentimento*] of immersion. The body, insofar as it is perceived as other, takes on a sense of its own reality, of its own effectuality, as an imaginary and pathic [*patica*] incision, as production of emotions and desire, to the point that the sensation of reality that is transmitted from the virtual environment depends in large part on the effectiveness with which it provokes emotions in the user.[43] From this point of view, "virtual reality can produce an experience capable of self-identification,"[44] but precisely as reality, that is, as alterity with respect to users, as environment in which one can act, as bodies that can be manipulated. Thus, the virtual body-environment is intermediary not only between computer model and sensible image, but primarily it is an intermediary between inside and outside. It is a strange place in which the border becomes territory, and whose ontological structure must be quickly articulated.

One of the most debated questions in contemporary ontology is, notoriously, the distinction between thing and event, and, relatedly, the distinction between concrete and abstract.[45] In virtual environments, what a user perceives as a thing is in reality an event, the temporary actualization of a virtuality existing only, in its present state, as a function of an interactive relation. This presses us to reflect on the necessity of considering in an articulate way the concept of "relation," and of reconsidering the notions of "thing" and "event" as relational nodes, without implying thereby any kind of drift, for the virtual in any case possesses an actuality of its own beyond that of the interaction (it is "real" precisely in being virtual). The issue is to articulate, at least briefly, the question of the object-event relation, to point out an ontological trait typical of the virtual body as defined here. Such an object-event relation has mostly been thought (if we decide for the sake of simplicity to neglect dialectical and neo-idealistic positions) as a form of relation between two values: the event is an object (or objects) that changes. Ontologies that admit of events often think of them as changes in an object, thing, or substance that is endowed with some form of permanence; then they conceptualize the event as relative to such becoming even when the object that undergoes becoming is not clearly identifiable. This is, after all, an outgrowth of Aristotelian ontology, which conceives of substance, with its intrinsic dynamism, as the principal category. From this presupposition the question arises of the symmetry between event and object and of the possible, conceptual dependence of the category of "event" on that of "object," even when one concludes that the two categories are not conceivable in separation. Now, the virtual body, while not reducible to representation, does not exist as body except in interactivity, *is* an interaction, an event-object [*oggetto-evento*]: an action (relation of interactivity) that is a body (virtual body) inasmuch as it possesses the characteristics usually attributed to bodies. The virtual body sustains itself in time throughout its changes of position, dimension, form, and color, but only under certain conditions related to its interactive nature, so that virtual bodies (as perhaps all bodies *simpliciter*) are (relatively) monotonous events—this is so precisely given certain conditions, though. Reflecting on such conditions leads, within the area that interests us, to the transformation of questions of the type, "Do things such as changes exist?" into questions of the type, "What are the conditions for the possibility of changes that are things?" [Such a reflection] therefore invites an analysis of the peculiarity [*tipicità*] of the virtual body (omitting for the time being the question of the ontological difference between virtual bodies and so-called real bodies). In the case of the virtual body, the event is an unrepeatable particular, a *concrete, yet subtle individual* (that is, an integrated system), constituted out of the interaction of a human body (thus a complex mind-body) endowed with technological prostheses, and an electronic processor implemented by an algorithm (in turn translated into a programming language). Now, does such a concrete though subtle individual occupy a single place? And if so, which place? Certain parts of my technological prostheses? Certain sensitive areas of my body? A certain part of my brain? A computer memory? It is, in any case, a body that admits other bodies into its place; it admits, for example, to having been traversed by my body, and if a virtual environment is a virtual body qualifiable as a structured set of navigable virtual bodies, then a virtual body can contain other virtual bodies within its own body: bodies that are within bodies, interpenetrating, like shadows, beams of light, angels, ghosts . . . [46] A virtual body occupies, assuming that these words have an intuitive sense, a certain portion of time-space, but not exclusively, as the virtual body happens within the time-space of a non-virtual body. Its temporal forms, moreover, are multiplied: what is its time? It certainly happens in the moment of interaction, but among its conditions of possibility, in its being a real body, there is the fact of having been previously written or recorded in a material support, in a memory.

Thus, a virtual body is and is not itself in time and place, as its self-eventuation, its becoming-event depends upon the interaction with a user. Now, can it be argued that reality is interactive *in the same way*? To this end, David Deutsch writes:

> What may not be so obvious is that our "direct" experience of the world through our senses is virtual reality too. For our external experience is never direct; nor do we even experience the signals in our nerves directly—we would not know what to make of the streams of electrical crackles that they carry. What we experience directly is a virtual-reality rendering, conveniently generated for us by our unconscious minds from sensory data plus complex inborn and acquired theories (i.e. programs) about how to interpret them.[47]

Deutsch's assertion is nothing but a form of transcendentalization of the empirical: what we *are* psychophysically conditions our "direct" experience of reality, that is, the constitution of a sensed [*sensato*] environment. Addressing the question would of course imply the positing of a theory of knowledge and an ontology. What is relevant here to emphasize is only that the virtual body *appears* to possess at least one quality that differs from those of the bodies that we usually call (on both the commonsense level and in the language of theory) "real." I would say that reality is not interactive in the same way as virtual reality is, and that "real" bodies are not events in the same way that virtual bodies are, inasmuch as the virtual body *more clearly* escapes the external-internal dichotomy than do bodies we consider real. Due to its discrete and interactive nature, the virtual body coincides with its history and is a process; yet it is not only the sum of numerically different phases—since the texture of the body depends on the interaction, it takes place as a sensed action for a subject and acquires its identity from such interaction. This identity, however, is relative, and thus it fluctuates consequently. Certainly any body, insofar as it is perceived by my body, is in a situation of interaction; however, as an object and as external, it appears as having the peculiar character of not being subjected to amendment; I cannot make it such that, *with a simple act of will,* an object is not in the way it is, that it is not what it is;[48] the external world would then be the non-amendable world, to which perceptual objects (which interest us here), but also those that are imperceptible, would belong. Now, from a theoretical point of view, the situation is different for the virtual body: even supposing that it is possible to separate a "simple volition"[49] from a movement or a perception, considering that virtual bodies would be, by means of sophisticated prostheses, directly connected to the sites of nerve impulses, there is nothing that would prevent a simple act of will from amending a virtual body. The question is, then, whether such an act is possible in its specificity only under the finite conditions included in the matrix, or whether it is possible to implement algorithms that allow a retroaction from the matrix, that is, a very powerful type of interactivity, and if so, in what sense: a program that learns, that modifies itself, and that develops within its relation to a user. Given the interactive nature of the virtual, I do not see why it would be theoretically impossible for this to come about, and therefore to produce a form of intersubjective communication mediated by computer memory, which would become, on the basis of a program, memory of experiences. Disregarding this possible development of the issue, it remains that if no-amendability is a necessary characteristic of the objects that belong to the external world, then the virtual body does not belong to that world. On the other hand, the virtual body is not a part of the internal world: the object-event of which it is constituted is neither my dream[50] nor my imagination, but an environment navigable by me and by others, a product of technology, and I remain aware of its difference with respect to what is usually called "reality" (which, as we have seen, cannot be perfectly simulated). In short, I would say that the virtual body is neither internal nor external, but is, if you will, an *outside-in* [*esterno-interno*], considering that this synthesis is not a mere sum, but is something else, that is, a testimony of the ontological novelty of the virtual body.

The virtual body, in its appearance, that is, as virtual, is its history, the history of its self-phenomenalization within a series of relations that constitute a virtual environment implying a human body endowed with certain prostheses. This pushes us to consider it as an event-object [*oggetto-evento*], which, in turn, can be interpreted at the level of ontology and with the related consequences either as a strange, relatively monotonous event that allows other bodies into its time-space, or as an event-object that extends over time according to a four-dimensional concept, or (in a partially Spinozian way, inasmuch as it supposes that time is an institution of reason and that the relations between event-objects—not between objects *and* events—are a form of immanent causality)[51] as a succession of instant-entities [*enti-istanti*].[52] This last position is interesting because according to it the permanence of the object in its dynamism is a cognitive illusion; this leads one to suppose that virtual bodies can be understood, besides as being discrete in space, also as discrete in time, that is, as numerically diverse temporal segments, and that their diachronic identity is potentially discontinuous.

2

My Body in the Virtual Environment

"PRESENCE" IN QUESTION

Reflection on the concept of *presence* within virtual environments has been unfolding for years,[1] and has seen contributions from scholars representing many different disciplines[2] with the goal of enabling the construction of environments capable of best simulating the complex sense of presence that constitutes our perceptive belief.

The objective of the research is a definition of "presence" that is a function of effectiveness: the sense-feeling, so to speak, of presence in a virtual environment is all the more interesting the more it is able to compete with the same "feel" in non-virtual environments, or as it is nonchalantly put, in "real" environments. The degree of illusion induced by the device is therefore what counts, and research is aimed precisely at the reproduction, or at the fiction of reality, and so on; obviously, this purpose guides the research. This desire goes on infinitely, as the designers of virtual environments know very well, and therefore it must be limited to an analysis of the degree of the user's attention: the more the virtual environment enables one to lose temporary contact with reality, the more pervasive and effective it will be. Thus, what is interpreted is the situation in which a user is set in a double environment, virtual and real, and is continuously able to focus his or her attention on one or the other. What needs to be encouraged is an immersion into the virtual primarily by means of relevant stimuli that serve to bind, to constrain, the attention. It has been suggested in this regard that presence in virtual environments should be considered as an illusion of nonmediation (a perceptual illusion of nonmediation),[3] and, relatedly, that nonmediation should be understood as disclosive of the degree of presence. But of course the quality of presence, taken as an indicator of the quality of the immersion and also of the interactivity, involves possibilities of action in the environment, expectations and adaptation, comprehension and dispositional attitudes, and thus outlines a field of remarkable theoretical density: "The experience of presence is a complex, multidimensional perception, formed by an intersection of (multi) sensory raw data and a variety of cognitive processes—an experience in which the factors of attention play a crucial role."[4]

One should therefore enter the speculative quality of this interweaving, which retains a conceptual depth that proceeds from perception to culture, and keep in the background the inescapable layers of complexity in order to evaluate their impact on a possible theoretical proposal.

The illusion of nonmediation can be a starting point because it requires, basically, the positing of presence as an immediate perception; the subjective feeling or sensation of being present in an environment is thus characterized by a quality of perception. The question then is to analyze perception within the virtual environment in terms of how such an environment is different, or means to be different from a mediated environment (and therefore from the perceptual qualities that overlap, on a second level, the perception of the environment, as it occurs in mediations such as film, television, photography), and from interactions that mediate the reading of texts or hypertextual navigation. In some respects, then, the question is simplified and the investigation may focus directly on perception:

> Once isolated from other similar phenomena on the basis of their differences, the question of presence relative to perceptual and interactive virtual environments inflects itself in terms of an analysis of the conditions for perception within these special environments. Note the reversal of perspective in comparison with the analysis carried out on the subject's sensations with respect to his or her location: the crucial point for the definition is no longer "where am I?", but rather, "what does it mean to perceive a virtual object?"[5]

In this way we situate the question within the context of simulation and assume that the task of the builders of virtual environments is that of perceptual conformity, so that a virtual environment achieves its objective if it can trick the user as to its status as "virtual." Now, the fact that the user does not distinguish, at the level of perceptual interaction, virtual body from "real" body, certainly does not per se entail

> that virtual objects are to be faithful copies of real objects. Emphasis is placed significantly on the interaction: it is the motor and perceptual conditions that must be similar, and not the properties of the objects represented, so that they can also be created worlds very different from the real, provided that they maintain an appropriate level of interaction.[6]

In this way, having overcome the problem of *mimesis* as true copy for the medium of perceptual analogies, the issue becomes one of objectivity as credibility: What makes an environment credible as an objective environment? More generally, "What is it that causes something (object, event, world) to be perceived as objective?"[7] The question is relevant, if one can manage not to loosen the perception-objectivity structure, because it permits an extension of the semantic space of the question of "presence." The answer cannot in fact concern only the sensible qualities of the environment or simply sensory evidence as criterion of credibility, particularly as criterion for the justification of perceptual belief; instead, such answer will exceed the physical conditions of the environment as conditions sufficient for the justification of belief in objectivity and will involve factors such as the success of the interaction within contexts of social recognition,[8] and therefore the symbolic and cultural components related to communication and cooperation.[9] Following the same strategy and returning to the question of perception from out of the results that have been indicated, we can then introduce the *affordances* of the ecological theory of visual perception so as to complete the picture; we will then attain an overall classification of the environment as a place of complex, subjective-objective[10] experience, at least relatively consistent with the users' expectations (which are always to some extent not only private but also dependent on personal "history") and projects,[11] and suitable for the exceptions that confirm the rule.

Now, the results of this approach are practically and technically effective for the construction of virtual environments; however, they presuppose the homogeneity of the ontological structures; they consider, that is, the virtual as a possible being and therefore as being in a relation of essential similarity and existential difference with respect to what is called real. In this way, none of the semantic fields (real, actual, possible, potential, virtual, and so forth) are problematized or revealed in their relation to one another, which makes the discussion less interesting from the speculative standpoint. The problem of perception in a virtual environment could be reformulated as: What can we learn in the philosophy of perception from a theory of "perception in virtual environments," given the specific nature of that environment? It is obvious that the discourse goes in circles, because it is always from theories elaborated in the field of the so-called real that we develop the difference, but it is a process typically philosophical, which, on the other hand, can make sense only if it can be shown that the virtual is an existent being that has (is) an ontological structure of its own. It is thus distinguishable by asking some elementary questions: What are the elements that make it possible for one to perceive a virtual environment? How are the subject-object difference and relation constituted within virtual environments? What does it mean, in short, *to perceive* a virtual object? The answer to these simple questions may emerge from an ontology of the virtual, which includes necessarily a discussion of the concept of the virtual. One should note that this does not take it as obvious that the concept of objectivity, related to that of object, has the same meaning for beings regarded as "real" as it does for virtual beings. If, for example, one thinks that an "external" entity or event is objective in the sense of existing independently of the (perceptual) experience that a subject can undergo, then the virtual "object" is not objective, even if one can say that this object exists beyond experience, or does not exist solely through experience. What, then, is the degree of reidentifiability of such an object? It will be partial and belong mainly to the part unidentifiable by spatial coordinates: not to the recurrence and constancy of form in diverse places, but to the partition of the object, that is, to the computer script. If, conversely, we believe that we can distinguish between perceptions or, more extensively, representations that show up as "external" and stable and representations that show up as "internal" in continuous adjustment through feedback mechanisms, then precisely our experience of the virtual body denies the possibility of the distinction. In fact, the multisensorial multiplicity of the input of virtual bodies is coherent and unitary because of the constancy of the link between property and place, as it cannot disregard the principle of noncontradiction (for which one single element from every class of perceptual property belongs in time t to the object in location l—note that one must assume the hypothesis still to be demonstrated, namely, that there exists a definable time-instant), and on the other hand, at the same time, the virtual body, through its interactivity, dissolves the difference between distal and proximal stimulus, insofar as it is, so to speak, both ontologically near and perceptually distant. A first step, then, is to consider the possibility that certain consolidated analyses do not work for virtual objects because of their status as ontologically different. It becomes then finally clear that the answer to the question of *presence* requires a clarification and deepening of the notion of virtual body-environment so that we can, circularly, show its peculiarities in terms of perceptual theory. I hope to arrive at this point, but it will take some time.

Now, when we speak of presence we can still accept an obvious [remark] well expressed in Husserl's phenomenology: there are no pure, uncontaminated data; every given is the result of a complex of intentional operations, and "all intentional unities come from a deliberate genesis, are 'constitutive' unities" [12] that are in relation with our past, with the history of our perceptual life, with the legacy of experience. Phenomenological description (the "static" aspects of phenomenology) has taught us to take into account, in our study of the structures of sense of *presence,* both the noematic and the noetic points of view. So, for example, from the noematic standpoint one will explain the relations, and in particular the relations of precedence in terms of validity, between the system of ghosts and the system of movements, and therefore of the deformations, of the partitions, and so on. From the noetic point of view one will inspect instead the differences between retention, recollection, expectation, and so on—in short, those modes of consciousness that are, for the phenomenologist, the conditions of subjectivity. The philosophical analysis of perception, which is normally an apprehension that intentionally embraces together all those layers that the analysis distinguishes, belongs, of course, to the phenomenological perspective. From here emerges a difference—obviously beyond that between the empirical and the transcendental scope of the analysis—between the psychological approach, which is pursued by scholars of the notion of presence within virtual environments, and the philosophical approach, which an aesthetics of the virtual cannot avoid, at least on a preliminary basis. Now a question might be: With respect to a virtual body, what changes, if anything, from the perspective of a phenomenology of perception? This is certainly not the only question one can ask in relation to the theme of presence within virtual environments, inasmuch as the phenomenological point of view is one of many possible philosophical ways of understanding *presence*; but it is a first question. This operation, which could now be carried out at least partially on the basis of experiences and case studies in terms of the theory of perception in virtual environments, could provide results that permit another question, which regards, circularly, the sense of the phenomenological method and its purpose. Well known[13] is the difficulty, not unlike the one that in Platonic theory concludes in the doctrine of recollection, regarding the relation between the historicity of the transcendental subject and the pretense of truth that results from the eidetic method: If in all perception is present, and it cannot be otherwise, the inheritance of a history of perceptual experience, almost like a passively established a priori essence that is a condition of the possibility of capturing the *eidos,* then we have a projection of the empirical onto the transcendental, of the historically constituted subjectivity onto the apprehension of world. Now "if the passively pre-constituted *eidos* that serves as a guide in the eidetic variation is, however, made up from a world with a specific ontological structure, *how can it claim validity for a possible world in general?*"[14]

This is a problem involving the constitutive ground of any representation from spatiality (and, more radically, from temporality) onward, as one can imagine, or at least not prejudicially exclude, cultural variations of the feeling of space. Moreover, the phenomenologist "is bound involuntarily by the circumstance that he takes himself as his initial example. Transcendentally he finds himself as the ego, then as generically an ego, who already has (in conscious fashion) a world—a world of our universally familiar ontological type."[15]

It is therefore always starting from "a world of our universally familiar ontological type," from a simultaneously obvious and necessary ontology, that eidetic fictions and variations are produced, and they will thus be limited in their freedom. Derrida has made the point;[16] beginning from the insuperability of the limit, he develops his program of research in the direction of "quasi-transcendental" figures. Certainly, an awareness of the limit of the freedom of variations and therefore, ultimately, of the limit of the imagination belonged already to Husserl who, proceeding on his way toward a genetic consideration, gradually increases his awareness of an essential perspectivalness. Of course, the transcendental ego is not empirical, is a functional center of intentional acts, is in and of itself prior to any worldly egoism, and puts aside the natural attitude linked to the psychological sphere. This is very important, as we shall see, even for an approach to virtual reality. In any event, it enables one to understand the particular curvature that the term *ontology* assumes within phenomenology and its relation with the term *world* (as the theme of transcendental phenomenology, the world, be it real or possible, is never an already given, a being present in the form of phenomena that contain an essence to be revealed, but is an eidetic complex that emerges through intentional operations. And ontology is, relatedly, the attempt to locate and describe layers of meaning of such world). Yet when the phenomenological project is no longer only descriptive, is no longer aimed only at identifying the essential differences among intentional acts, but becomes a search for "what works in subtle, subliminal ways, what is absorbed and metamorphosed in the passive synthesis,"[17] and when the power of the imagination correspondingly emerges as internal to the genesis,[18] then there also emerges the question of the limits of that power:

> Can I imaginatively make it so that my body is transformed into that of my childhood, and my mind into that of a child? Isn't this by all rational accounts a kind of nonsense? With these questions we see that the problem of the changing of perspective [*Umdenken*] has not been properly raised or treated.[19]

It is no coincidence that the issue of "changing perspective" is central in Sartre and Merleau-Ponty, that is, in those authors who have developed their own ways of phenomenological research, devoting great attention to the dimensions of opacity, implication, lack of purity of the *cogito*, in short, with a renewed attention to the body, and therefore to the historicity, affectivity, emotions, and, conclusively, the perspectival materiality of the ego. The typically transcendental research into the invariable structures that *should* be found as common to the different conceptions of world is thus not interrupted but rather complicated and problematized.

At issue here is a revision, present in Husserl himself,[20] of transcendental subjectivity in the direction of corporeality as a condition of possibility for any objectual apprehension. What is important to stress is, however, the further development of the question because of the complexity and novelty of the virtual field. In other words, if we hold fast to the methodological lesson of phenomenology that leads to an exercise of the imagination as variation with the goal of capturing the transition from the emergence of forms, from the variety of images, to the identity of objects and their essential meaning; and if we think of this experience not only as a typology or empirical description of the field but as an analysis of its stratification, since we consider the field as an ontological territory made of material layers; and finally, if this account is possible only at the level of intentionality, then the fact that, in the case of the lived experience belonging to virtual images, the subject's body is necessarily prosthesis-equipped and the object's body is an eminently interactive hybrid may have consequences that impact the phenomenological method's claims to transcendentality. Can one still speak of a generic ego, "who already has a world—a world of our universally familiar ontological type," when there no longer exists a "familiar ontological type," or when the ontological type is no longer so "familiar"? Abstractly, with respect to the object one can ask: What happens when the intended object is not a body, not an image, but rather is a hybrid image-body [*corpo-immagine*], and yet it is not such a hybrid in the very same way as a painting, a photograph, a movie picture, a television image is, at least insofar as it does not have the same intersubjective quality, a quality that is always connected to the degree of interaction? I will return to this point below, but for now I note that the degree of interactivity implies a difference that impacts the very possibility of experience. And what point of view, what perspective should we assume for the inquiry? The perspective of a split egoism, both internal and external to the virtual environment? Are we perhaps getting close to a paradoxical situation such as to call into question the possibility of a "common sensing"? Obviously, this leads us to consider the question from the point of view of the constitution of the aesthetic object, where imagination and image play in an inextricable circularity. For now, though, I have only posed a problem: the issue is to engage the question of *presence* in the virtual environment while holding firm, in a manner not too naive, to the essential phenomenological advantage that accounts for the complexity of processes. The question that then arises is this: How important is, in the analysis of presence within the virtual environment, the *necessary gap* with a perfect simulation? It should also be noted that the analysis of the field (a field of interacting forces, in our case consisting of users and virtual bodies) cannot be a merely verbal description of the contents of a user's experience, even if that user is the subject making the description, precisely because language attributes to the contents of experience an awareness that might not be legitimate. The issue is rather that of unfolding the layers of the genetic history that has led up to a specific experience, of retrospectively showing its development, of grasping the dynamics of its constitution, but without the pretense of universality that the technological development radically forbids.

Equally abstractly, on the side of the subject one must take into account the inorganic prostheses that come to constitute the "body" of the operator-consumer-actor in the virtual environment. This is relevant for the phenomenological tradition, and to me it seems to point in the direction of its further deepening, and not to a denial of its method. Let us take up the question from some distance: Who or what is the "subject" that "feels," that is, that perceives and understands? It is not a disembodied mind, it seems, but an inextricable mind-body complex. To be sure, this is what Merleau-Ponty has progressively taught, first stressing the factor of the body, and then developing the strange and complex notion of flesh as an environment of organic-inorganic participation. But the simplest—or at least most primary—approach to the question arises from the consideration of the user's body as a body with inorganic clutches that make it possible to perceive and, in part, to constitute, virtual bodies. This body is "a cybernetic organism, a hybrid of machine and organism, a creature of social reality as well as a creature of fiction."[21] Post-human theory indicates "new ways of living out identities through a mutating body, never finite or definite, a hybridization of the organic and inorganic, between biology and technology, between flesh and circuits."[22] We can understand it conceptually as a figure of the limit and the surpassing of the limits between organic and inorganic, and, more generally, between nature and artifice:

> Matter continuously becomes something other, the inorganic insinuates itself into the organic; in the organism we find the machinic, but never anything simple, original, ultimate. It is a concatenation of the infinitely small, a concatenation

of heterogeneous fragments. Strata. The conscious organism is a provisional aggregate, a temporary suspension of information particles, of matter, of desire, in movement towards self-disintegration.[23]

But for our purposes the body in a virtual environment is simply a "structural coupling,"[24] a prosthesis-body [*corpo-protesi*] that belongs to the project of recomprehending the "functions of the organism within a machine's encoding,"[25] that enhances the body's ability on the one hand, and on the other develops the skills of the machine through the prosthesis of "the organic body." One will need to question what the consequences of this are at the phenomenological level and also at the level of an ontology of the artificial.

It is now necessary to reflect with care on the following point: we cannot simply hypothesize that the body endowed with inorganic prostheses corresponds, in virtual relations, to the living body or the body proper[26] as described by the phenomenological tradition. Perhaps, as Nancy writes, "we shouldn't think the 'ontological body' except where thinking touches on the hard strangeness of this body, on its un-thinking and unthinkable exteriority."[27] It is true that bodies "take place at the limit, *qua limit*: limit—external border, the fracture and intersection of anything foreign in a continuous sense, a continuum of matter. An opening, discreteness. . . . The body is the place that opens, displaces and spaces phallus and cephale: *making room for them* to create an event."[28] It is also true that "the between-bodies is their images' taking place."[29] And in particular, "the *image* (that it [the body] thus is) has no link to either the idea or, in general, to the visible (and/or intelligible) 'presentation' *of* anything at all. The body's not an image *of*. But it's *the coming to presence*."[30]

All of the above functions, and we therefore take advantage of it, as a description of the immersive and interactive virtual field. Yet, the issue is not thinking the negation of the living body as much as it is thinking of the body that comes from inorganic integration *as* of a living body. Yet, it is not a matter of thinking of the nonliving as organic, but of thinking of the inorganic as living without thereby making it be animated. What is at work here is an intentional, nonobvious modality. What certainly disappears is the hierarchy of mere body-objects on the one hand, which would exist *partes extra partes,* and the living body on the other as a condition for "having a world." Also lacking is the idea of the body as a space of appropriation, as that which can be inhabited and directed from within. Abandoned, therefore, is an internal-external difference more profound than the essential internal-external involvement that only the concept of the living body enables us to think. Also suggested, moreover, is the possibility of an overcoming of the univocal relation between consciousness and identity that developed from the theory of the living body as an organon or schema of self-consciousness. In sum, self-consciousness is consciousness that is traversed by the world and that restores the world.[31] Examples, it seems to me, of experiments that proceed in this direction are the operations of Stelarc and perhaps the last performances by Antunez Roca.

Since the distinction is a matter of views or intentions, the organic-inorganic body synthesis can be considered *at the same time* as living body, and as body-object, an aggregate of extended parts that carries out biological functions and is thinkable and describable in physical terms. The notion of body qua machine is no longer indicative of reductionism. The cyborg is a complex made up of the psychophysiological and the physical, the mental and the machinistic, the natural and the artificial, the organic and the inorganic. As such, it is a vehicle for expressive possibilities in the virtual environment; the cyborg is precisely "our general medium for having a world"[32] in the virtual domain. Now, after having indicated the direction in which to think of the body as endowed with technological prostheses, we can rewrite it in the terms of the *Phenomenology of Perception*. Structurally an intentional aperture, a taking in of the world that establishes itself in the opening movement, such a body is not a mere object and cannot be grasped in its complexity through an objectifying gaze. Therefore, it is always imminent to any scientific approach and stands rather as the condition of possibility of a descriptive language. It is "the horizon latent in all experience and itself ever-present and anterior to every determining thought,"[33] a *preobjective view*[34] able to perceive its own movement as an event within the environment, a complex of affective and kinesthetic sensations, a "body schema,"[35] a spatiotemporal complex *in situ* that determines the very existence of the environment's spatiotemporal characteristics. This is a body that, because it is a condition for the possibility of experiencing an environment, itself constitutes that environment. It is an embodied consciousness that arises primarily not as an "'I think that' but [as an] I can,"³⁶ that takes the environment as a set of possibilities for action, of expressive possibilities constitutive of qualitative horizons.

In the virtual environment, the user-body inhabits the space and time that its interaction constructs as specific virtual space and time, and in the interaction it phenomenalizes the virtual body-objects that constitute the environment itself. The technological prosthesis seems to confer upon the body an extraordinary power, which in non-virtual environments is the effect of habit, of repetition, "the power of dilating our being-in-the-world, or changing our existence by appropriating fresh instruments."³⁷ It is the power to assimilate otherness into one's body, making it an expansion and an expression of one's own time-space so that the body's perceptual and cognitive activities constitute the very field of presence as a set of meanings. In other words, in the dynamics of virtual relation, or of the constitution of the virtual environment, the peculiar relation between a body equipped with prostheses and a virtual body is such that meaning is internal to perception, or to that encounter which we continue to call "perception." I will return later to this delicate point; supposing, however, that in the virtual environment—understood in the strong sense that we have defined—relations between users by means of avatars are possible, then it will be the case in such an environment that, as "the parts of my body together comprise a system, so my body and the other's are one whole, two sides of one and the same phenomenon; and the anonymous existence of which my body is the ever-renewed trace henceforth inhabits both bodies simultaneously."³⁸ The *other* user-body, as virtual, will be, strictly speaking, a hybrid and paradoxical body. I realize that this body is hardly conceivable in its perceptual and imaginative dynamic, inasmuch as it is difficult to think of the outside gaze that is the condition of objectivity. This is, however, the most complex case because it presupposes the possibility of a relation between identity and difference in which a relation to three positions is reduced to a relation to two positions due to the assimilation, in the avatar, of the body equipped with prostheses and the virtual body: this is an identity among diverse elements that at the same time remain as such. At this level, the perceptual environment most similar to that of the virtual, at least with respect to the complex and immediate feeling of presence, is perhaps that of dreams.

WHAT DREAMS TEACH US

Without a doubt, we are made of the same stuff of which dreams are made, and perhaps our lives are immersed in a great sleep. It seems to me[39] that Leibniz was right to claim that it is not "impossible, metaphysically speaking [that is, for Leibniz, speaking in the language of truth], for a dream to be as coherent and prolonged as life."[40] Now, the nature of dreams has been studied in the last twenty years or so by cognitive psychologists according to its paradigms,[41] and, consequently, has been thought in relation to the mental activities of perception, reasoning, and the production of narratives.

> In classical cognitive perspective . . . one thinks that there are interesting relationships between dreams and interaction with the world. . . . This is easily understandable when one considers that classical cognitivism conceived of perception, thought, and action as mental, autonomous and separable subsets, and of action more specifically as the ballistic performance of specific instructions, recovered from an internal catalog and put into effect in advance amidst a process of reasoning . . . guided by an explicit purpose.[42]

Going beyond this formulation, we can challenge another presupposition, namely that:

> The dream is something radically external to the mind, in the same sense in which the images we perceive or the stories to which we are audience are external to us. Classical cognitivism draws a clear ontological difference between the procedures that are supposed to constitute the mind and the information (collected from the environment or recovered from the sheds of memory) on which these procedures would operate. What is characteristic of the mind are the procedures, while the information is mere contingency. And because the procedures are understood as rules in a formal system and are explicated, as we say, in the third-person . . . the theme of *presence,* of the *participation* of the individual in an ongoing situation, is in last place among the interests of classical cognitivism.[43]

Recently, dreaming has also been examined, in researches within the psychology of consciousness,[44] as an altered state of consciousness (similar to hypnosis and sensory deprivation). This means a move beyond the hypothesis of a computational mind, which circulates in various forms of cognitivism, toward an inquiry broadly phenomenological, which presupposes neither the existence of an external order to which a family of meanings objectively belongs, nor the possibility of a mind observing such an order from the outside. Further, in those studies that take into account aspects of the mind such as the experience of the self,[45] the rootedness in the experience of the body or embodiment,[46] the interaction between cognition and action, and between cognition and social world,[47] dreams have been characterized "as a particular kind of conscious intentional activity."[48] We can now take advantage of this definition, which implies the negation of some ways of thinking about dreams (e.g., as perception without stimuli, as the generation and comprehension of "external" stories), allowing for the consideration of them in light of their specific quality of *interactive presence,* even beyond the question as to whether they are altered states of consciousness.

Now, the dream, according to this interesting perspective, is a *unilateral* construction of interaction.[49]

> In the dream, however, the coupling with the real world is clearly weakened: the fact is that the mind does not interact with the real world (whatever that really means), but with a fictional world that it builds for itself moment after moment for the facilitation of interaction. . . . The dream is therefore a peculiar form of consciousness in which, in the absence of the world (with which we maintain a weak but important contact), we individually and unilaterally give rise to the conditions that constitute the experience and creation of meaning.[50]

I prefer to withhold judgment on unilateralism, not only because it suggests some assumptions that require discussion (the assumptions that there is consciousness as a center of intentional acts, that such acts are interpretable as *representations of* something and at the same time interactions *with* something, and that the representation is a *point of view* that in turn means the possession of consciousness, that is, the translation of being conscious into self-consciousness), but mainly because the notion of unilateralism depends upon a clear distinction made between the real world and a fictional world. Now, without presupposing a complex system of interpretation it is difficult to draw a distinction between the internal and the external, and still more between the real and the fictitious, or between the private world of consciousness and the external world of reality. Such a distinction resists even when it is mitigated by an intentional structure. In this regard, I prefer to embrace decisively the Cartesian position,[51] and in a radical way: We have no tools, with the exception, *perhaps,* of the complex construction of a metaphysical system, so as to distinguish dream states from waking states. In short, there is no external perspective that can distinguish between the two states in such a way that the distinguishing operation itself is guaranteed not to be internal to the dream. So while on the one hand I assume the distinction without being able to demonstrate it, on the other I prefer to diminish (in ways that will be seen) its degree of unilateralism, precisely because the unilateralism seems so obvious (is it not *I* who is dreaming?). In brief, I believe that if we avoid thinking of the self as ego, as a more or less decentralized yet in some way creative [being], and instead conceive of it as an interactive function, then we may be able to bring together some suggestions and construct an analogy among forms of *presence.* But we still have to go some way before we reach this result. The "sensation" of *presence* is indeed a peculiar characteristic of dreams: dreams are environments in which we participate in an immersive manner, in which we are not spectators, but actors. They are environments in which we are not observing or generating events as stories, in which we do not have the impression of the duplicity of the gaze, as if assisting in a show.[52] We also know that the feeling of *presence* in a dream is sometimes more powerful and pervasive than in waking. This force of presence has been explained precisely as a result of the unilateral nature of the interaction. The environment understood as "external world" is rich with calls to action and the possibility of perceiving minute details while remaining aware of the background and its complexity.

> In the dream, conversely, we move in an environment unilaterally reconstructed in order to facilitate interaction. What this world must contain is only that which serves the ongoing interaction—and, in fact, this is about all that it does contain. In the absence of a real world acting as external memory, the creation of a *surplus* of world with respect to what is necessary

> for the interaction is limited to the capacity of our internal memory. . . . The vividness of presence in the dream is probably due to this (relative) poverty of the oneiric world: instead of having to be busy with and worry about the rich variety of *affordances* that characterize the real world and divide our capacity for presence . . . we spend all of this capacity on those few features of the world that we can unilaterally create.[53]

With the positing of the connection between unilateralism and poverty of the fictional world of dreams, one could also explain the relative *incoherence* intrinsic to these worlds:

> To unilaterally create a complex world is difficult, but it is more difficult still unilaterally to maintain its coherence over time. . . . The problem is that the mind is made to keep up with changes in the world, not to create them from scratch or from chaos. Whereas the novelist maintains and constantly updates an external memory (a canvas, a set of notes) to help him keep track of what happens to the characters and the world in which they move, the mind immersed in a dream can appeal only to its own internal memory resources and capacity for prediction. No wonder if it encounters difficulties in carrying out this task, or if these problems come about in the form of gaps or inconsistencies in the plot.[54]

Perhaps we can explain those very same traits that belong to dream experiences (immersion, intense quality of *presence,* incoherence) and avoid the hypothesis of unilateralism; dream aspects could simply depend upon the constitutive interaction between the subject's avatar and a dynamic memory, which precisely belongs and does not belong specifically to the subject, or belongs to it while exceeding it in several directions, so that the dream world would be a complete integration of subject and environment. Memory here means anything but a storehouse of images or events, or a set of traces; it indicates, in the words of Edelman, "a principle underlying the evolutionary development of mind and intentionality. . . . Memory, in this sense, describes aspects of inheritance, of immune reactions, of reflective learning, of genuine learning, which follow the perceptual categorization of the various forms of consciousness."[55]

Thus, memory is not a static archive to be consulted, but a plastic and dynamic complex in which different models and levels of interaction are integrated and amalgamated. Memory is a condition for the possibility of action and nonreproductive performance on the part of the body well beyond mere subjective awareness. We are here talking about memory of the species, fundamentally adaptive; memory as a source of meaning and generation of analogies, that is, of the constitution of models according to similarity of properties or constraints such as to orient actions. Memory, in this sense, "is not a component of the mind, but is instead a global property of our mind."[56] It is probably the case that in the waking state, memory so defined is engaged or "secured"[57] in the world through perception, not in the sense that previous experience interferes with current experience determining or constituting it as a conceptual scheme,[58] but rather in the sense that memory becomes a system with the actual experience, which is often resistant and has the ability to surprise and contradict expectations, and determines [such experience] bestowing it a sense that can only come about in the structure of relation. Mingling with the present, memory can suspend the primacy of the latter and imagine possibilities of actions. But here we are interested in remaining within the dream, in which the difference between internal and external memory (or the world) fades because the very difference between inside and outside disappears. In other words, within the dream, memory—which is more than just a link to the world or to a world storehouse—is both what belongs or is intimate to the subject, and what is other, alien, different, and therefore capable of causing surprise, stupefaction, and at times anxiety. Now, the highest property (beyond immersivity, intensity of presence, and relative narrative incoherence) of the dream, itself a place of interactions that is structurally interactive, is its heterodirectionality. Is it not true in fact that we know that we are *not* the directors of our own dreams? Do the bodies and events that show up in our dreams not appear as immutable, as if they were other to us? Do we not know that we *cannot* change the appearance of the dream by a simple act of will? The dream, its material components, and its causal development escape the constructive grip of the avatar. We are, in short, at the mercy of our dreams, so that what, when we are awake, seems to have been unequivocally an "internal" experience has been lived as the experience of an uncontrollable "exterior." One should notice that I do not suppose any, however obvious, distinction between conscious and unconscious, if only because it would imply a topology that I cannot justify. Instead, I merely point out an experience of heterodirectionality that I assume to be common. [Such an experience] probably implies that the dynamic memory that constitutes, as it were, the stuff of dreams is also composed of desires of which we are unaware in the waking state; briefly, that [such a dynamic memory] is an uncontrollable (even) emotional fabric. But this is not what interests us at the moment. We are interested in trying to capture some similarities and differences between forms of memory and environments, between the dream and the virtual. In the dream, we experience our being odd subjects: we are ourselves and at the same time representatives of ourselves, that is, avatars; we are fully immersed in a world which only from an impossible, external point of view is considered fictional, but which is in fact maximally real to the point of producing a sense of *presence,* that is, a particularly intense perceptual quality of otherness or heteroaffectivity. This world is constituted in the interaction between avatar and memory; such memory is not poor, but rather endowed with considerable density and reach, at least to the extent made possible by the potentialities of one's cerebral connections. Now, conceiving of the dream as of an avatar-memory interaction in which the two terms are both the same and different, as of an environment-structure that integrates subjective and objective, inside and outside while still respecting their distinction, allows us easily to interpret the typical characteristics stressed above, namely, presence and incoherence. The dream is incoherent only with respect to the presupposition of a unitary and subjective director. In our everyday relation with the world we tend, almost out of necessity, to construct narratives out of events that perhaps have no sense of unity, and we tend to duplicate the subjective gaze by transferring it outside of our own affairs to the point that the mind seems to narrate spontaneously, perhaps in order to construct some meaningful order or sustainable environment. But this does not happen in dreams, and it is clear that within them the director of the story, assuming that there is one, is not us. In other words: dreams are not in themselves incoherent, but are understood as such as a result of the exigency for coherence of the narrative mind, itself probably constructed as an adaptive, self-increasing, teleological function. This also explains the intensity of *presence,* as this is connected, at least in part, to what provokes attention and the subsequent pressure for response, to the gap that causes amazement, to the encounter with an unpredictable visitor, or with the familiar that sometimes shows its face in shadow. Therefore, the perceptual qualities peculiar to dreams not only show with clarity the difference between stimulus and perception, let alone the lack of necessity for an external body in the generation of perceptions of otherness, but above all and most interesting for our purposes, they also demonstrate the significant density of an environment made of a structure of relations, an interactive environment that allows for a revision of the difference between thing and event, object and image. In fact, what we perceive to be a body within the dream is really an event of memory, and also what we conceive of as a body is a mental image, that is, if you will, an image of memory. So too, though more basically and with some differences, in the case of the virtual environment. It should be clear, however, that the differences are relevant: the virtual environment is constituted in interaction with machines, and the understanding of this situation would preliminarily demand a theory of the artificial.[59] Georges Simondon has spoken of the "inter-individual couplage" between human being and machine. This "couplage," for Simondon, "begins to exist from the moment in which a code common to two memories can be discovered, so that a partial convertibility from one to the other can be achieved in a possible synergy."[60] This environment seems to be made of nonmimetic image-bodies [*corpi-immagini*], event images, and not images *of* something else, even if the mimetic relation seems to belong to the nature of the image. It is time to untie this knot.

3

Forms of Expression

MIMESIS?

There is no crisis of mimesis except the one occurring on the surface.[1] We know of the semantic amplitude of the term, which cannot be reduced to a process of imitation, and which, in certain theoretical frameworks, has come to mean the fundamental structure of human desire.[2] Mimesis is at the crossroads of mechanical and creative representation, and it traverses the meanings of similarity and expression, simulation and assimilation. Mimesis is the territory in which the process of the aestheticization of the world is currently being played out, triggered by uncontrollable currents of mimetic desire and the discovery—and sometimes the protection and caretaking—of novel resemblances that open up horizons of meaning. Mimesis is now a field of hybridization between the sciences, from anthropology to technology, from the human sciences to ethology, and in this connection what is here interesting is the further mutation brought about by the novelty of the virtual body. As has been noted,[3] mimesis is not only a cognitive process, but is also a doing/producing that involves the participation of the body, which appropriates the world in a particular way through the mimetic process. Therefore, this process is resistant to theory and open to a double historicity related, on the one hand, to the becoming of the organic body as reorganized in its perceptual and cognitive potentialities through inorganic prostheses, and on the other, to the becoming of the object that makes itself virtual as synthetic image. This means that the field of the virtual can be seen as a relational environment, that is, as a set that includes mimetic processes, because of its intrinsic character of internal-external process, of construction of intermediary space. The notion of mimesis can thus become an interpretive tool of the virtual environment and the interactions that constitute it.[4]

The process of making-itself-similar (to reproduce, imitate, or represent), which constitutes the meaning of the mimetic act already in pre-Platonic sources, yields to a dynamic of nonconciliatory synthesis between production of meaning and fiction, between believing and make-believing, between being and making it be. Now, the virtual body is a product, a thing or object, that potentially can be mistaken for something analogous but with different characteristics. Such an analogue may be the object of imitation, so that the virtual body can serve the function of deception or deceptive fiction. Yet, as virtual object, it has its own characteristics that cannot be reduced to the result of a deceptive imitation, but that rather configure it as a form of mimetic modeling, that is, as production of a symbolic model based on a relative isomorphism with respect to its analogue. So, if a relation of resemblance belongs to any mimetic class, it is the relation between similarity and difference that distinguishes such specific classes; virtual bodies, due to the peculiarity of this relation, constitute a class of their own. One can say, from the point of view of the aesthetic and artistic properties of the virtual body, which for now we leave undetermined, that a mimesis capable of adhering fully to the paradigm such that it disappears into it in complete participation is not a good one. Nor can we say that the alternative between good mimesis (figurative) and bad mimesis (fantastic) can be determined through the relinquishment (or lack thereof) of the awareness of the character of appearance of one's own being, that is, of the awareness of one's being mimesis; the virtual body is *both* original *and* copy, and in no case a forgery of the truth of the original. And if it creates an illusion, such an illusion is still not far from the truth. In other words, the virtual body is not a mere copy even when it originates from processes of disclosure in synthetic images of non-virtual bodies. This is so because [the virtual body] is not to be understood in relation to that which it represents, its meaning is not a re-identification with the original, it does not suppress itself as if it were a means, it does not amount to being a means, it does not exist for self-effacement; rather, it exists so as to act as an entity endowed with a particular relational structure capable of opening up new perceptive, imaginative, and cognitive possibilities.

Moreover, even a painting seems to entertain a peculiar relation to its possible being as copy. Even a painting, like any analogic or digital image, is an image-thing [*cosa-immagine*] in a more or less mimetic sense. We can, for example, reflect on the ontological value of a painting-image [*immagine-dipinto*], understood in simple and traditional terms as a representational-mimetic form, and then work by means of difference. Gadamer, as we know, articulates an ontological model for this:

> In our analysis of the concept of the picture we are concerned with two questions only. We are asking in what respect the picture (*Bild*: also, image) is different from a *copy* (*Abbild*)—that is, we are raising the problem of the original (*Ur-bild*: also, ur-picture). Further, we are asking in what way the picture's relation to its *world* follows from this.[5]

One should recall that the analysis develops from a consideration of mimetic processes, of the "transient" arts in which "the world that appears in the play of presentation does not stand like a copy next to the real world, but is that world in the heightened truth of its being."[6] In these processes, mimesis does not indicate "a copy so much as the appearance of what is presented. Without being imitated in the work, the world does not exist as it exists in the work. It is not there as it is there in the work, and without being reproduced, the work is not there."[7] Now, with respect to paintings, added to the question of representation is the issue of the image, which also includes the position of a different concept of mimesis: "Thus, the concept of the picture goes beyond the concept of presentation (*Darstellung*) used hitherto, because a picture has an essential relation to its original."[8] On the other hand, the advantage obtained is not lost, because even with respect to the picture "one cannot say that reproduction is the real being of the work. On the contrary, as an original the picture resists being reproduced."[9] The essence of a picture, as image, does not consist in being a copy, in functioning as reference to something else, but rather in the composition of a certain bond with what is represented that respects at the same time both similarity and difference. It is a specifically aesthetic differentiating bond by which the image is constituted as a being of its own, as a being of representation: "This kind of picture is not a copy, for it presents something which, without it, would not present itself in this way. It says something about the original."[10] The subsequent theoretical move proceeds beyond the claim of the autonomy of the image and affects the ontological dimension of the original: "That the picture has its own reality means the reverse for what is pictured, namely that it comes to presentation in the representation. It presents itself there."[11] Of course, the original can be said in many ways, but the fact that it came to presence in a *specific* image now belongs to its being: "Every such presentation is an ontological event and occupies the same ontological level as what is represented. By being presented it experiences, as it were, an *increase in being*. The content of the picture itself is ontologically defined as an emanation of the original."[12]

For Gadamer, the most exemplary place to look for this proposal is the religious image, inasmuch as it seems to have an "ontological communication" with the represented. In Gadamer's view, however, nothing prevents a similar argument from applying to mimetic image-things produced by "modern techniques" such as, in the first place, photography and the cinematic image: "Even today's mechanical techniques can be used in an artistic way, when they bring out something that is not to be found simply by looking."[13]

I would say that compared to all this, the virtual body goes one step further, carrying its relation to non-imitative mimesis to extreme consequences. Of course, in the event that one tries to define the image as a mimetic relation, one can modify the original-copy relation by stressing the ontological value, the autonomy, and subsistence of the image as representation: "For strictly speaking, it is only through the picture (*Bild*) that the original (*Urbild*) becomes the original (*Urbild*: also, ur-picture)—e.g., it is only through the image that what is represented truly becomes something that gives itself in an image."[14] But in the case of the virtual body, thing-being is in no way separable from image-being, so that the idea of vicariousness, of vicarious presence, proper to the concept of representation, tends to be reduced until disappearance. What increases is instead the idea of power, which, as Gadamer points out,[15] is intrinsic to that of image. Before being an image-of, the image is in fact power of signification that precedes what is signified. In this sense "every picture is an increase of being and is essentially definable as representation, as coming-to-presentation."[16] This ontological increase in the virtual body, whether a synthetic or a structural image-thing [*cosa-immagine*], belongs however only secondarily to what is represented; in the first place, it belongs to the virtual environment. In fact, if the virtual body is mimetic, then it is mimetic in the same fashion as any formative process is; as a body, it represents itself, it is not representation but appearance, yet at the same time, as image, it is representation. One should notice that unlike paintings or other analogic images, in the case of the virtual body one cannot distinguish thing (for example in the abstract form as a support) from image. This is so not because a material structure cannot be identified, but because it is in the interaction that the image-body [*corpo-immagine*] phenomenalizes itself, happens as a body, and comes to appearance in its support. As such, there is no before or after this process, there is no autonomous self-persistence as a matter-form synthesis, or as a self-sufficient meaningful expression. The fruition does not come about only as an interpretation or positing of meaning; rather, it is in itself constitutive of the image's body-being [*essere corpo dell'immagine*].

Now, let us consider this relation of fruition as a relation to what a certain system of values has understood as works of art, and thus, as grounded within a varied but recognizable tradition. We should then think of aesthetic appreciation as devoid of *distance*, which has been a condition for the possibility of the significant form of artistic value, and should instead think of it in terms of a kind of *suction*, of the entry on the part of the consumer into the body of the work and at the same time an entry of the work into one's own body or imagination. This involves an accentuation of the pathic and total dimensions of the relation: [it is a matter of] my becoming one single body with the work, which undergoes the effects of my presence and which, through the changes produced by this undergoing, in turn modifies my feeling. Now, one might read some artworks as approximations to this extreme idea, or one might illustrate how such an idea acquired an attractive power for the poetics of some artists, who are always in fact collective authors, or of some groups. I limit my examples to some works that are very well known. One of them is Charlotte Davies's *Osmosis* (1995),[17] a space—which Oliver Grau has defined as non-Cartesian—in which, thanks to certain prostheses, we move through breathing ("to go up, breathe in; to go down, exhale"), and which has stirred much debate and can be retraced by reference to Pierre Lévy's beautiful description:

> In slow motion you penetrate the world where you were born, crossing layers of cloudlike computer code, winds of words

and phrases, until you finally land in the center of a clearing. From now on, you direct all your movements. Awkwardly at first, then with greater assurance, you experiment with this strange new way of moving. Breathing in sharply, you rise above the clearing. Small animals like fireflies, dancing on the outskirts of the forest, serve as your escort. A pond covered with water lilies and strange aquatic plants glitters before you. The world is soft, organic, dominated by an omnipresent vegetation. Leaning over, you head toward a large tree that appears to serve as the axis of the sacred clearing. Suddenly you come into contact with the tree, penetrating the wood itself. As if you were a sensate molecule, you follow the channel used to carry its sap. Breathing in sharply, you rise inside the tree until you arrive at its topmost branches. Surrounded by capsules of chlorophyll, soft green in color, you enter a leaf, where you watch the complicated dance of photosynthesis. Leaving the leaf, you hover again above the clearing. You drop down to the pond by exhaling heavily and again cross a swarm of fireflies (sprites?) that give off a strange sound like bells ringing in the distance. Turning your head, you watch as they fly toward the forest, accompanied by the lingering echoes of the fading sound of celestial bells. Now you are nearly on top of the surface of the pond, where you stop to watch the play of reflected light. As you break through the water's surface, a fish, undulating gracefully, welcomes you to the aquatic world.[18]

Relevant to the pathic substance of interactive art are the installations by Studio Azzurro, from the 1995 *Tavoli (perché queste mani mi toccano?)* [*Tables: Why Do These Hands Touch Me?*] up to at least the 2002 *Le zattere dei sentimenti* [*The Rafts of Feelings*]. Of *Tavoli*, Andrea Balzola writes the following description:

> Six wooden tables arranged in a dark place are "set" with video-projected images: domestic images, such as a candle, hands that prepare a tablecloth, a portly woman, a bowl, a loaf of bread. . . . Visitors are invited to touch these surfaces, but while living an experience singular and surprising: are they touching the materiality of the table [the six tables are made of wood] or the immateriality of the figures that occupy it? The

action of touch causes (through a system of invisible sensors) a micro-event: the bread is removed, the candle sets fire to the table, the woman slips from the table, and so on.[19]

Le zattere dei sentimenti is, as affirmed by Studio Azzurro,[20] a "journey of feelings" in which viewers can, by touching, in different ways, interactive boards to which shipwrecked survivors desperately cling, help or hinder the salvation of the interactive images.

Any work of art is such only in its fruition and interpretation, but this concerns the sphere of meaning and its definition, which is certainly multiple and prone to being infinite. Relation to it (literally) aside, however, [the work of art] remains as mere thing, as supply, as *presence* potentially at hand and endowed with some abstractly enumerable phenomenal qualities. Conversely, the virtual body emerges as such only in interaction. Therefore, its essence is not simulacral. Nevertheless, by presenting itself it represents and puts at stake a non-imitative sense of mimesis. In order to see how this can happen it will be helpful, before returning to the question of the meaning of mimesis and representation, quickly to examine the question of the simulacrum, and therefore, of the image.

REPRESENTATION?

As will be recalled, I claimed that the digital image is not simply an image-of[21]—is not simply a mimesis of a thing or of an image, and therefore is not essentially simulacral. Nor, for that matter, is it an icon or original image; rather, it is to be understood as a peculiar genetic-relational form. Thus, the digital image, at least in its strongest characterization, is not strictly speaking "image" but "*subtle* body," a hybrid image-object entity, and its appearance, its existence as image, is essentially interactive. Let us now justify these observations, first of all in their effects with respect to some traditional categories in aesthetics, namely, representation and simulacrum.

When the virtual body is understood as representation, it demonstrates a unique complexity and paradoxical nature. In what sense, for our purposes, should we understand the term *representation*?

If we reflect on the nature of representation, we certainly find in Nelson Goodman the most radical critique of its being understood in terms of resemblance or reference justified by similarity according to a sign-signified relation. For Goodman, even realistic simulation

> is a matter not of any constant or absolute relationship between a picture and its object but of a relationship between the system of representation employed in the picture and the standard system. . . . Realistic representation, in brief, depends not upon imitation or illusion or information but upon inculcation. Almost any picture may represent almost anything; that is, given picture and object there is usually a system of representation, a plan of correlation, under which the picture represents the object. . . . If representation is a matter of choice and correctness a matter of information, realism is a matter of habit.[22]

Goodman's position, which proposes radical conventionalism, constructivism, and ultimately nominalism,[23] thinks the difference among symbolic systems by means of a theory that distinguishes depictions or pictorial and graphical representations from linguistic descriptions and musical representations as the difference between non-notational and notational systems, which, in turn, is based on the difference between the discrete and the continuous, digital and analog. Now, for Goodman, if they are correlated to a field of reference that permits a semantic interpretation, the syntactic conditions, that is, the conditions of syntactic disjunction, finite syntactic differentiation or articulacy belonging to a symbolic, notational scheme give place to a symbolic system, which is in turn notational insofar as it satisfies the semantic conditions of nonambiguity, semantic disjunction, and finite semantic differentiation. According to Goodman, a symbolic notational scheme is a syntax and therefore a set of discrete characters, that is, separate and continuous, that correlates to a field of reference segregated in the same manner, so that each character isolates its object and vice versa, thereby giving rise to a semantic notation: for example, a musical score such that it allows implementation without the possibility of variations. It is clear that this is an extreme idea, and the difficulty of the proposal consists in finding examples that allow the connection between syntax and semantics, or between schema and notational system.

In this theory, natural languages are clearly syntactic *schemes* but not syntactic *systems,* whereas computer language is an interesting element to be explored. It does not matter, one should note, that the characters of the system are numbers (digits). What matters is that a digital schema is completely discontinuous and that its characters are bi-univocally correlated to classes of congruence in an equally discontinuous set. It is also necessary that the system be completely differentiated both syntactically and semantically. Hence the definiteness and repeatability that digital devices can provide. Now, a digital image that is not *properly* modifiable in an interaction, not exactly interactive, might exemplify a semantic interpretation of a symbolic scheme. We would have then the opportunity to clarify beyond any process of resemblance the difference between an analog and a digital image, even when, paradoxically, the digital image "represents" the analog picture, or possesses the same "content." The digital image would then be a representation that is not a mere depiction but a description, as opposed to the painting, which is not a notational symbolic scheme, but rather one that is syntactically dense inasmuch as it fails to permit a finite scansion of the scale of values that belong to it. In other words, the painted surface is a potentially infinite continuum of characters, which does not allow for a finite semantic differentiation. This has consequences for the overall description-depiction difference, painting as a representational system, and other specifications involving the virtual.

In general, we have confirmation of the refusal of resemblance as a criterion for distinguishing between representation and description, whose difference has no ontological dependency:

> Descriptions are distinguished from depictions not through being more arbitrary but through belonging to articulate rather than to dense schemes; and words are more conventional than pictures only if conventionality is construed in terms of differentiation rather than of artificiality. Nothing here depends upon the internal structure of the symbol; for what describes in some systems may depict in others. Resemblance disappears as a criterion of representation, and structural similarity as a requirement upon notational or any other languages.[24]

In turn, this "disappearance of resemblance" implies a structural uniformity among syntactically dense symbolic systems, such as graphical diagrams or paintings. A structural difference between description and depiction is only a difference of degree between representations:

"Though the pictorial and diagrammatic schemes are alike in not being articulate, some features that are constitutive in the pictorial scheme are dismissed as contingent in the diagrammatic scheme; the symbols in the pictorial scheme are relatively *replete*."[25]

It is therefore only the degree of syntactic saturation that distinguishes, among semantically dense systems, those that are, let us say, more representational. All this, finally, leads us to recognize

> the full relativity of representation and for [the possibility of] representation by things other than pictures. Objects and events, visual and non-visual, can be represented by either visual or non-visual symbols. Pictures may function as representations within systems very different from the one we happen to consider normal; colors may stand for their complementaries or for sizes, perspective may be reversed or otherwise transformed, and so on. On the other hand, pictures when taken as mere markers in a tactical briefing or used as symbols in some other articulate scheme do not function as representations.[26]

This frees the notion of representation from that of a depiction of the world, from any impoverished conception of mimesis, from the idea of copy and simulacrum, and opens up a space for the symbolic construction of worlds, almost ushering in a profound idea of multimedial synaesthesia.

Yet the consequences implied by the consideration of the digital image and, as we shall see, of the virtual body, give rise to the suspicion that things are not so simple. We denied that the relation between analog and digital image can be based on a relation of resemblance, on a perceptual relation, or on a phenomenal given. Goodman is very clear about this, and demonstrates well that a diagram can be either analog or digital. Although apparently one can assimilate them to analog examples "because of their somewhat pictorial look and their contrast with their mathematical or verbal accompaniments,"[27] we must remember "that the significant distinction between the digital or notational and the non-notational, including the analog, turns not upon some loose notion of analogy or resemblance but upon the grounded technical requirements for a notational language."[28]

Now, if this means that "the often stressed distinction between iconic and other signs becomes transient and trivial"[29] and thus allows for "the full relativity of representation and for representation by things other than pictures,"[30] then one must also admit, on the contrary, that the description can be made with images, as in the case of the digital image. It is not only pictures that can function as representations within systems very different from what to us "happens to look normal," but also within systems of description other than those to which we are accustomed. We could therefore have a symbolic vehicle that is not syntactically dense for "art" that is, so to speak, figurative. But, we might ask, is it not evident at this point that we are excessively forcing the language of theory? In the theory of notation proposed by Goodman, can depiction be truly brought close to description? The criterion of distinction is clear: a symbol can function as representation if it belongs to a representational scheme that is sufficiently syntactically dense. Things become even more complicated if we consider the virtual body as digital image-body, or as hybrid image-body: this is, of course, the self-phenomenalization of an algorithm in binary format, that is, a syntactically differentiated symbolic diagram, and it concerns the scope of exemplificative experience, which involves properties expressed and not simply denoted. But it is not possible in this case to repeat the existing relation between score and performance, in the first place because the virtual body is also image and thus depicts, but also because in our case the interaction intervenes, or can intervene, on the score itself. One should notice that the interaction constitutive of the event-being [*ente-evento*] is an interaction between the discrete and the continuous, between, so to speak, an analog system, a mind-body complex endowed with prostheses, and an algorithm exemplified by these data points that come to saturate perception. It thus seems to me difficult to read the virtual body in terms of Goodman's powerful theory of notation, and this is evidence of the virtual body's peculiar novelty. This does not imply a direct rejection of the theory, its assumptions, and its consequences, but it seems difficult to extend its scope to include the virtual body. Among other things, virtual art could not be interpreted as either autographic or allographic because it both *depends* intrinsically and at the same *does not depend* intrinsically on a notation, and even the famous "symptoms of the aesthetic" theory, which for Goodman as well does not claim to be exhaustive, should be modified.

To be sure, Goodman has taught us a lot: he has demonstrated well that what we call "world" always happens within complex conceptions of the given:

> [T]here is no innocent eye. The eye comes always ancient to its work, obsessed by its own past and by old and new insinuations of the ear, nose, tongue, fingers, heart, and brain. It functions not as an instrument self-powered and alone, but as a dutiful member of a complex and capricious organism. Not only how but what it sees is regulated by need and prejudice. It selects, rejects, organizes, discriminates, associates, classifies, analyzes, constructs. It does not so much mirror as take and make; and what it takes and makes it sees not bare, as items without attributes, but as things, as food, as people, as enemies, as stars, as weapons.[31]

Analyzing the antiquity of the eye, ear, and hand, approaching the density of particular symbolic worlds, and clarifying common misunderstandings about the symbolic function of various art forms, which basically depend on the use of a naive notion of resemblance or of the correlation between representation and likeness, are only a starting point for an operation whose aim is to learn to construct symbolic worlds. Goodman articulately defends an epistemology characterized by the rejection of any separation between perception and conceptualization, and thus also of the separation of observation from theory. The refusal of the epistemological priority of "*Elementarerlebnisse*" has been matched by an equally clear rejection of the a priori. This means that constructional formal systems "may be founded on many different bases and constructed in different ways,"[32] since all meaningful references to a world are always characterized by a system of description or depiction. On this basis, even incompatible systems, such as physicalism and phenomenalism, "do not necessarily conflict, but may be regarded as answering different problems."[33] Now, to maintain that ontological claims are considerable as true only in relation to the modalities with which they construct their objects, only in relation to "ways of seeing" the world, does not mean a reduction to subjective truth, but rather a complication of the logic of truth and its distribution across different levels. The being of worlds, their truth, is plural, and thus many worlds, not just one, are true, but at different levels of structural complexity. This openness appears as ontological relativism only to those who believe not simply that the world is something other than its construction, but especially that the construction is something other than the world. Methodological pluralism, I think, cannot be mistaken as ontological relativism, and its problem is not that of reference, but of the distinction among various truth-values contained in different versions of the world. In short, Goodman merely argues that reference to the world is meaningful only within a symbolic system, and that symbolic systems that are different and even mutually incompatible as for their interests and problems at hand may nevertheless be well constructed. This leads to a further analysis of the characteristics of symbolic worlds that appear, in their novelty, on the horizon of our experiences. If the interpretations made possible by given symbolic systems do not seem, with regard to their novelty, sufficiently explicative, this only testifies to the historicity of experience and its interpretations.

SIMULACRUM?

That images produced by the new media are to be understood as simulacra is a well-known and interesting theory that enables a reading of the complexity of the contemporary. It has its precedents in the 1920s in Lippman's category of the *pseudo-environment*, a mixed environment comprised of reality and image in which social actors are embedded and play their roles, and had a significant development with Boorstin in the early 1960s, at a time when the pervasive power of the media seemed to dissolve social and educational reality and make its events *pseudo-events*, that is, media productions that were primarily intended to meet their own intrinsic purposes. The conceptual framework of "simulacrum" has allowed us to interpret the pervasiveness of the media image and the related processes of the aestheticization of reality. Now, "the simulacrum is not a pictorial image that reproduces an external prototype, but an image that actually dissolves the original."[34] Its connotation implies thus a theory of the origin and of mediation with the origin, of its representation. This introduces teleological and metaphysical themes into the discussion of the process of spectacularization.[35] The simulacrum would in this sense be a concept that allows one to go beyond the dimension of iconoclasm as well as that of iconophilia, both to some extent related to the search for an archetype. A subterranean metaphysics of the origin, that is, a cult of the original not unlike the cult of the icon would be concealed, even in the demand for, or at least the expectation of, an image-reality media relation that is so realistic that it can coincide with reality, even in the criticism of media manipulation, that is, of the constitution according to devices of hyperrealistic images that are faithful to a preimagined hyperreality. The simulacrum on the contrary "is neither icon nor vision: it does not have a relation of identity with the original, with the prototype, nor does it imply a laceration of all appearances and the revelation of a pure, essential truth. The simulacrum is an image without prototype, the image of something that does not exist."[36]

So the simulacrum is an "almost nothing," a synonym for an idol condemnable as such, both for iconophiles and iconoclasts, because "for them the right to fix a correct line of demarcation between true and false images, between icons and idols, constitutes an essential premise, a guarantee of identity."[37] The simulacrum speaks of the overcoming of a tradition that focuses on the idea and the sensible copy of the idea; thereby, it opens to an intrinsic historicity of the image, freed from metaphysical burdens and from reference to the dignity of the archetype.[38] Not even the simulacrum becomes the original, thereby assuming the claim to autonomy of the artwork. This autonomy, too, positing itself as original and therefore metahistorically valid, only serves to shift the emphasis away while still remaining within a theory of reference.

> The concept of the simulacrum instead implies the rejection of an external prototype just as much as it does the rejection of a temptation to view the image as prototype: it is thus connected with techniques for the industrial reproduction of the image. . . . The concept of the simulacrum, understood as an artificial construction devoid of an original and unable to constitute, like the a work of art, itself an original, finds the conditions for full implementation in contemporary mass media.[39]

In light of all this, it is clear that the notion of simulacrum can be a powerful interpretive scheme. Despite this, however, the simulacrum, the image *without* identity, the image that *does not* possess an autonomous originality, cannot avoid establishing itself, ultimately, as a negation of originality, and from this negative trait it takes on the character of an albeit non-nihilistic fiction. Even in Baudrillard's version, which exhibits the simulacrum-simulation connection[40] in order to differentiate simulacrum from representation as related to the myth of the origin, the negative trait remains:

So it is with simulation, insofar as it is opposed to representation. Representation starts from the principle that the sign and the real are equivalent (even if this equivalence is Utopian, it is a fundamental axiom). Conversely, simulation starts from the Utopia of this principle of equivalence, *from the radical negation of the sign as value,* from the sign as reversion and death sentence of every reference. Whereas representation tries to absorb simulation by interpreting it as false representation, simulation envelops the whole edifice of representation as itself a simulacrum.[41]

So the simulacrum is not a masking or distortion of reality, is not a masking of the absence of reality; rather, it is privation of any relation to reality. Even in such precise and extreme connotation a remainder, namely, the process of negation, becomes manifest, which casts the simulacrum in a dialectical relation with the origin, and thus in a symbolic process. In order to avoid restoring a metaphysics of difference between the true world and the apparent world, this heaviness of the origin will be pushed back indefinitely in a typical mimetic process of removal. After all, if by "simulacrum" one understands a mimetic relation or resemblance in which the original is infinitely retracted (and I think that this process is internal to the concept and intrinsic to the meaning of the term), then the structure of the simulacrum is built on the structure of mimesis: a deferment without the original, but where the origin or model remain as absent with no real (albeit claimed) annulment of the idea of origin or of relation to the origin as model.

I think this is well understood by Baudrillard, as evidenced by the evolution of his thinking. Initially, as we have seen, the concept of simulacrum emerges from that of simulation, understood as that which governs the relations of exchange, production, and consumption, through the elision of reality: a swapping of signs with no intervention, in the exchange, of "something real."[42] In this phase of theoretical production, value is at the same time set and annulled in the exchange as "symbolic," in an indefinitely reversible relationship in which the symbolic "is neither a concept, an agency, a category, nor a 'structure,' but an act of exchange and *a social relation which puts an end to the real,* which resolves the real, and, at the same time, puts an end to the opposition between the real and the imaginary."[43] As we know, the difficulty of the paradoxical concept of symbolic exchange, impossible to think in its destabilizing charge because of its oscillation between salvation and destruction of subjectivity, is consequently replaced by the notion of seduction, the stylistic production of appearance, wherein "to seduce is to die as reality and reconstitute oneself as illusion."[44] But finally, after exploring the territory of seduction, Baudrillard, in a further untiring attempt to escape the traditional conceptual dichotomies of the philosophical tradition, examines the notion of illusion, almost as a residue or resistance to the virtualization of reality. Of interest here is a brief and specific line of this criticism—certainly not comparable to situationism, or to Debord—of society living in the "ecstasy of communication":

> Virtuality is different from the spectacle, which still left room for a critical consciousness and demystification. The abstraction of the "spectacle" was never irrevocable, since we are no longer either alienated or dispossessed: we are in possession of all the information. We are no longer spectators, but actors in the performance, and actors increasingly integrated into the course of that performance. Whereas we could face up to the unreality of the world as spectacle, we are defenseless before the extreme reality of the world, before this virtual perfection.[45]

It is clear that the concept of the virtual staged here has a very broad meaning indicative of a complex process of the medial absorption of reality. The issue is that of the substitutive mediation made possible by high definition:

> The key concept of this Virtuality is High Definition. . . . Everywhere, High Definition marks the transition—beyond any natural determination—to an operational—formula—and, precisely, a "definitive" one, the transition to a world where referential substance is becoming increasingly rarer. . . . The high-definition image. This has nothing to do with representation, and even less to do with aesthetic illusion. The whole generic illusion of the image is cancelled out by technical perfection. As hologram or virtual reality or three-dimensional picture, the image is merely the emanation from the digital code that generates it. It is nothing but the desire to ensure

that image is no longer image. It is precisely what removes a dimension from the real world.⁴⁶

Now, it is very clear that this position rests on the virtual-real dichotomy, and also on the Sartrean notion of image as process of de-realization and therefore as opening up of freedom, which presupposes a distancing from reality made possible only by positing the difference between real and imaginary. The theory, or as it were the theoretical hope, elaborated in *The Perfect Crime* is acceptable for its critical import, and it can be effectively absorbed if one eliminates the presupposed dualism sustaining it. This operation arrives at the specular result of the theory: that is, *not*, as Baudrillard writes, at the elimination of reality, referentiality, otherness by way of the virtual : "That of the world that is annulled with Virtual Reality. . . . No more illusion: hyperreality, Virtual Reality,"⁴⁷ *but* precisely the converse: at the ontological level, the lesson of the virtual image-body is the discovery of reality as a scheme of illusion and vice versa, the circularity of reality and illusion, or the truth of the secret of illusion: "If there is a secret to illusion, it involves taking the world for the world and not for its model. It involves restoring to the world the formal power of illusion, which is precisely the same as becoming again, in an immanent way, a 'thing among things.'"⁴⁸

To arrive, however, at an affirmation of the power of illusion as the opening up of worlds within the world as a distinctive property of the virtual requires a rather lengthy journey. For now, there is an advantage to which we can at least provisionally attest, namely that insofar as digital images manage to escape the mimetic dynamic, they do not have a simulacral essence. Perhaps one can achieve the same goal by emphasizing the relation between simulacrum and communication, the virtual and perception, so that the virtual body insofar as artificial is identified by "a technology that first has realized, explicitly and programmatically, that experience is not of reality, but of the relation to reality. Its novelty lies in its being the first medium that does not communicate messages, but perceptions of the world."⁴⁹

From this consideration it can be argued that:

Theories of the simulacrum observe the media's capacity to produce a certain kind of extra-medial reality by following the needs of their own communication. In a radical version like that of Baudrillard, they even claim that this pseudo-reality or neo-reality tends to replace true reality itself, to remove and annul it. But in the first place the nature of electronic pseudo-reality is that of a real experience, that is, of a new reality that is not superimposed or interposed between the subject and an alleged "other" reality, but rather becomes part of the environment and of the experience of the subject.[50]

It is now a question of following a double movement, which is necessarily circular in exposition, of further analysis: on the one hand it is directed toward the image, on the other toward the concept of the virtual. Their intersection will then be demonstrated in the specificity of the virtual image-body [corpo-immagine].

4

Toward the Image

As has been noted, the concept of simulacrum is dependent on a mimetic structure of the image in which the latter is ontologically dependent on something other than itself. It is always conceived as image *of,* such that to be image means to resemble some other. If this is so, then the issue becomes that of understanding further the various ways of deferment, similarity or dissimilarity, representation, reference, relation with, to, or of the model. This raises certain questions: Is it true in every case that the image is not to be original? Is it true that "the image is always inseparable from an understanding in terms of parentage?"[1] In order to approach the image, to grasp its meaning, must one always implement a cognitive process conducive to the discovery of its origin? Must one do so in order to come to nature, to the idea, to the divine, to all original forms of things that are independent from being known through images, in order, ultimately, to reach the world, be it the hyperuranian, this beautiful family of herbs and animals, or the unconscious, which is unknowable except in its figures? In this case, the image would be a reality that exits itself and becomes other than itself, alters its shape, so to speak. The birth of the image would thus be reduced to a matter of kinship, which may or may not be seen as a distancing and alienation, or as a manifestation of meaning and display of richness; yet, it would remain unavoidably symbolic, the recognition of a unity forever lost. But of course all this must have a cause: Why does the doubling occur, with its inevitable betrayal of both resemblance and difference, through the transcendental, historical, or psychological mechanisms of translation? This and nothing else, that is, the problem of the double, is of course the problem of truth as conformity [*adeguazione*]: the doubling of reality in the order of the other, which has its origin in the image as representation and in the image as imitation. The question of the image is thus a theological question and regards the meaning of the analogy of being: things resemble God because of their perfection, because every perfection or essence represents-reflects its own paradigm in God, who is the source of all perfections, be the divine an impersonal, ideal place (which a lesser god mimes or expresses in the process of becoming) or a mind as realm of possibilities. The order of perfections reflects and vaguely represents the unity and simplicity of God, but everything, to the extent that it is, is in God's image. All things—above all, the transcendental unity of multiplicity—represent God. In its transcendental sense as totality of all existents, the world, which transcends totality as mere sum of entities, is an *imago dei* [an image of God]. The concepts with which we signify God are figures of figures, representations of representations, which mark relations of distance and proximity, lines of truth and holiness, of error and sin, of morals and metaphysics, which for the situated observer split apart, but in reality are a single line. In the grand mimetic strategy, the difference between thing and image is shattered via participation and commonality: if things are images of the divine, then God is present in all things, is really ubiquitous, since God is in things insofar as they participate in being, and the similarity of the image is measured by the way of being of the entity, by the extent of its participation, which is always participation in the act and thereby in the causal efficacy of the divine. The divine exists in things and things exist in God, in the name of the image. In this light, many systems appear similar beyond the immense variability of their mimetism, mechanical rather than genetic or expressive.

IMAGE-BODY AS EXPRESSION

The mimetic structure, which is just the reverse of the participatory or creative dimension, leads to a thinking of the thing-image complex as an inextricable weaving. This is something reminiscent of the monad as conceived by Leibniz. In Leibniz's grand narrative, a drama that at the climax of the *Theodicy* becomes the story of a dream,[2] the monad is the actualization of a tendency to existence, of a desire to exist, which occurs on the basis of an extremely complex program, a grand calculation of maximum and minimum, perhaps self-contradictory, but in any case infinitely extended both intensively and extensively, made from a mind that is both matrix and programmer. From this point of view the universe is, overall, a virtual production, as Deleuze has noticed: "[T]he world or the hazy line of the world resembles a virtuality that is actualized in the monads. The world has actuality only in the monads, which each convey it from each monad's own point of view and on its own surface."[3]

Now, the concept of the monad conceptualizes a body entirely sui generis, a peculiarly subtle phenomenon-body [*corpo-fenomeno*] that is at the same time representation and represented. It is representation insofar as it is expressive power and it is represented insofar as it is properly body, that is, limit or passive margin of the expressive power. The monad is in fact both activity and relative passivity as a lower degree of activity, because only the active force or power accounts for a nonpartial multiplicity: multiplicity is a degree of activity, that is, of expressivity. Thus, and this is for us a point of maximum interest, perception and apperception are to be thought of as expression. Leibniz writes: "[T]he multiple finite substances are nothing other than diverse expressions of the same universe according to diverse respects and each with its own limitations. In this way each substance has an infinite iconography."[4]

The *subtle* body of the monad is the limit of its expressivity. The monad is a metaphysical principle of the physical world through the medium of the mass-energy and energy-expression equivalence, in its own way or in the way of its limit, that is, in the way of the program by which it is generated. Such a function of representation phenomenalizes itself, assumes a "body" by unfolding its significance as a determinate monad in degrees of perception, or more precisely, in the degrees that from the perceptual unconscious lead to the conscious unfolding of the apperception. Thus, the monad comes about as a perceptual-expressive action, which is certainly an interaction with respect to the matrix (which for Leibniz is the divine mind), with respect to the program that is the condition of possibility for the monad's own perspective. As we know, Leibniz does not think inter-monadic action possible due to the absolute simplicity of the monad: the monad is a partial-whole or a whole-part, and the inter-monadic *connection* consists only in the preestablished harmony of the program:

> Just as the same city viewed from different directions appears entirely different and, as it were, multiplied *perspectively*, in just the same way it happens that, because of the infinite multitude of simple substances, there are, as it were, just as many different universes, which are, nevertheless, only perspectives on a single one, corresponding to the different *points of view* of each monad.[5]

Yet one can say that in reality there is no city-object, a universe-object multiplied by points of view, as if such viewpoints might circumscribe it through adumbrations that can never exhaust it. Because the universe aggregate is monadic, then the root of the compound, its truth, is the simple. It is thus the city itself, the universe itself, that perceives—infinitely multiplying its own perceptions—the very same viewpoints that perceive it: "This interconnection or accommodation of all created things to each other, and each to all the others, brings it about that each simple substance has relations that express all the others, and consequently, that each simple substance is a perpetual, living mirror of the universe."[6]

One should notice the powerful metaphorical construction: a living mirror is a subject-mirror, that is, a subject-object that represents both objectively and subjectively. It is a paradoxical point of view, insofar as it is a coincidence of itself and the universal, which defers itself infinitely. It is a *mise en âbime* of perspective: perspective on perspective infinitely. Perspectival representation and expressivity are linked to the cognitive modalities of the monad as constitutive conditions of the world, so that experience is in no way separable from its being. Here emerges the problem of the monadic body, which cannot be understood *only* as a well-founded *phenomenon*. The issue, related to interaction as the condition of possibility for the self-phenomenalization of an entity, is crucial for a theory of the virtual body. It is the problem, which is present yet not solved in the last phase of Leibniz's production,[7] of the limit or margin, that is, the classical metaphysical problem of the "thisness": How can one delimit that which characterizes *this* monad, its precise expressivity, its point of view, its *body*? What is, in short, the reason for the precise and focused opacity of the body? Why, if the body carries with itself an essential confusion, does such confusion (or monadic unconscious) seem to be structurally disharmonious? This is the problem of the body-image bond, of the perspectival limit of expression. It seems difficult that this limit may be identified in activity, inasmuch as the activity that each monad is has its own limit precisely in its own body. Now, the body of the monad is a residue that does not allow activity to be thought of as perspectival expression resolved in reflection, in purely internal mirroring; rather, in order to be itself, it implies and posits a *minimum of exteriority*, a relation of interactivity with respect to a source other than the matrix. Deleuze describes such a minimum in the following manner:

> Leibniz discovers that the monad as absolute interiority, as an inner surface with only one side, nonetheless has another side, or a minimum of outside, a strictly complementary form of outside. Can topology resolve the apparent contradiction? The latter effectively disappears if we recall that the "unilaterality" of the monad implies as its condition of closure a torsion of the world, and infinite fold, that can be unwrapped in conformity with the condition only by recovering the other side, not as exterior to the monad, but as the exterior or outside *of* its own interiority: a partition, a supple and adherent membrane coextensive with every-thing inside. Such is the vinculum, the unlocalizable primary link that borders the absolute interior.[8]

Deleuze captures the difficulty well, but not the consequences, because the contradiction is not "only apparent." One must then go farther and think of the monad as an interactive image-body complex, as a model of an inside-outside hybrid, a hybrid of body and image, in short, as a virtual body.[9]

We must now try to think of the image-body [*corpo-immagine*], of the image-body bond at the ontological level so as to reach a point where we can consider "image" as the *proper name* of the virtual body. If "image" refers to imitation, then this seems to imply anteriority and posteriority, an essential split between primary and derivative. But let us try, by performing a thought experiment, to project the question, so to speak, *in divinis*, that is, in a logical space devoid of *prius et posterius* [before and after].[10] It is then conceivable to think of the image as an essential imitation of the species, of the form, such that it does not involve *posterioritatem, sed solam assimilationem* [posteriority but simply assimilation]. "Image" would then be the *proper name* of the virtual body, because the latter proceeds from the program in such a way as to remain immanent to it and vice versa. This is true insofar as its *ratione* is the *similitude speciei* [resemblance of species] of that from which it stems. The term *image* in fact expresses this absolute resemblance, since the image-being does not depend on the degree of similarity, but on the nature of the procession, on being a procession *ad intra* through resemblance, a process that remains immanent to its principle while expressing it in difference as difference, or, in a circular manner, a procession of the principle as image, because [the principle] implies the being of the image as its own expression. Now, the virtual body qua image specifies itself as a being that is the convergence of a double procession, as the summit of a double encounter: it proceeds from both the prosthetic body of the user and the programming language: a double-procession of the image, or image-body; not imitation, not representation, but mimesis. One can also say that the virtual is a real relation: a relation of procession, or a relation between a generator and a generated, which is body, that is, individual[ity]. This is a strange ontology: an individual, this individual, with its peculiar features or qualities, which is relation and nothing other than relation. It is a matter of communicative time-space,[11] both corporeal and mental, that is, an *experience* that should be investigated in its specific traits.

BEYOND IMAGE CONSCIOUSNESS

What happens when what is perceived is an interactive image? Let us begin with an examination of Sartre's analysis of the mental image,[12] which is to be understood as a rather unorthodox phenomenological investigation, yet to my mind very acute in its methodological naiveté precisely as it lends itself to an essential critique:

> In order to liberate the image from perception, Sartre suddenly reduces the image to the form it takes on in a de-realizing, or better, un-realizing, imagination. Sartre therefore excludes not only that the image can coexist with the perceived object, but that it can perhaps connect with the substratum of the object or even participate in its constitution.[13]

Now, I think Sartre has good reasons to support the position that is here criticized, reasons, however, that do not apply if one is referring to the virtual image-body. Let us try to understand on what grounds.

The virtual field makes the first obviousness immediately collapse:

> In no case could my consciousness be a thing, since its manner of being in itself is to be *for itself*; for consciousness to exist is to be conscious of its existence. It appears as a pure spontaneity, confronting a world of things which is sheer inertness. From the start, therefore, we may posit two types of existence. For it is indeed just insofar as things are inert; their inertness is their safeguard, the preserver of their autonomy.[14]

In the case of the virtual environment, however, simple and decisive oppositions do not work, the active and the passive are not duplicated, and one is not the reflection of the other. The virtual body is no mere resistance, inertia, or barrier to activity. As we know, the space of difference is established for Sartre at the level of the imaginary, that is, at the level of that way of being that is existence as image, and that is different from factual existence or existence as thing. Existence as image has the same nature that belongs to the existence of consciousness, and at the same time, circularly, it is the condition for the possibility of that existence. And it is, we should notice, an individuated existence characterized by qualitative specificities, in its own way concrete yet unique, such that it is not the reproduction of a more or less weakened impression. It is not, in short, a type of existence that can be confused with that of perception. The mental image would have a different ontological structure than the perceptual image: there is a hiatus, perhaps even a chasm, between mental and corporeal, which then in Sartre becomes stabilized as the fracture between in-itself and for-itself. Now, this essential accomplishment of Sartre's theory does not work for the virtual field: the virtual body is an image-thing [*cosa-immagine*] hybrid precisely in the sense that it sums up the ontological confusion between mental and perceptual image. On the wave of the problems that emerge from Sartre's position, let us try to clarify the ambiguities of the relation between body and image, that is, the difference among mental image, body, body that is image, and image-body [*corpo-immagine*]. Firstly, it is clear that the image present in the mind that is imagining consciousness is not a copy of an object, and that the mind is not a screen that is perforated by the percept or on which the percept inscribes or projects itself. Thus, the image cannot be analyzed as if it were a thing. In other words, images are not visible *for* the mind or *for* consciousness, they are not a psychic *state,* but rather the mind's global way of being, like memory, and this prevents an infinite duplication of the look. The image is therefore neither interiority, which would be opposed to exteriority, nor inferiority, a diminished copy or anything of that kind. In other words, for Sartre, image-being is an intentional modality:

> By becoming an intentional structure the image has passed from the inert conditions of consciousness to the consciousness of a synthetic relationship with a transcendent object. The image of my friend Peter is not a vague phosphorescence, leaving the perception of Peter as a footprint in my consciousness, but is a form of organized consciousness, in its way referring to my friend Peter in one of the possible modes of intentioning Peter's real being.[15]

What happens, though, if my friend Peter is a virtual body? Or the avatar of my friend Peter? Surely what matters is the mode of intention. The problem is, however, that in the case of the virtual body the *object* would not exist phenomenally, and thus noematically, if it were not *my own*, so to speak, image. Thinking the difference between percept and image is therefore difficult. Perhaps this means that the difference between perception and image is not original, or in any case not immediate, or is not a phenomenal given. In fact, for Sartre image-consciousness is consciousness in its unrealizing function, which has its noematic correlate in the imaginary:

> Consciousness of this sort is immediately distinguished from all others because it is presented to reflection with certain signs, certain characteristics that quickly determine the judgment: "I have an image." The act of reflection, then, has an immediately certain content, which we call the *essence* of the image. This essence is the same for all men. The first task for psychology is to define it, describe it, fix it.[16]

Now, in a virtual environment, that is, in the virtual-body or virtual field complex, not only is a transcendental level not granted since the ontological type of the various relational entities is not clear ("familiar"), but also the judgment "I have an image" as being distinct from "I have a perception" is debatable. It is not clear *what* one can denominate as "image," because the object, precisely insofar as it is constituted intentionally, is structurally ambiguous. Thus, in our case, it is not true that "what is conventionally called image is given immediately as such to reflection," and it so happens that perception and imagination converge rather mysteriously.

Sartre's analysis is certainly useful for eliminating some presuppositions that are in a broad sense naturalistic: "We had thought, without even realizing it, that the image was *in* consciousness," or: we had thought "that the object of the image would have been *in* the image," and so "we had pictured consciousness as a place populated by tiny simulacra: images."[17]

This pushes us to reflect on the meaning of the immanence of the image, and thus break up the relation of resemblance in the event that such [resemblance] is understood as belonging to the nature of the image:

> When I say I have an image of Peter, they think that at this moment I have in my consciousness a certain picture of Peter. Such a picture would be the object of my actual consciousness, and Peter, the man of flesh and bone, would be touched only indirectly, in the most external way, solely in virtue of the fact that it is he who is depicted in the portrait.[18]

Sartre also points out clearly how perception too is an intentional modality, and how the difference between perception and image is articulated at the level of intentionality:

> When I perceive a chair, it would be absurd to claim that the chair is *in* my perception; according to our adopted terminology, it is a certain modality of consciousness, and the chair is the object *of* this consciousness. Now I close my eyes and produce the image of the chair that I just received. The chair, which is now offered as an image, certainly could not enter into my consciousness more than it did before,

and therefore

> An image of a chair is not and cannot be a chair. . . . Whether I perceive or imagine this chair, the object of my perception

and that of my imagination are the same: it is always the straw chair on which I am sitting. Simply put, consciousness refers to the same chair in two different ways.[19]

Yet, Sartre's system rests on a rather subtle internal-external opposition: it presupposes the existence of an entity (the chair on which I sit) to which consciousness refers according to different intentions.[20] Such an entity is reduplicated: it is there outside of consciousness, there partially (there-and-here as perception), and it is here, on the internal screen of the mind (as image: now I close my eyes . . .), certainly not *in* but *as* consciousness, according to its modalities. Be it percept or image, the reference is to an individuality that in the first case is encountered in the world, that is, in a minimum of exteriority, and that in the second case is not, inasmuch as the minimum of exteriority or the outside that should be thought of as a condition of the encounter, that is, of the perception as intentional modality, is annulled. And, as is well known, for Sartre image consciousness amounts precisely to a de-realizing function: that is, consciousness as imagining nullifies the object, performs an un-realizing or de-realizing operation with respect to the residue of externality, to the elsewhere that indicates space, body, matter, resistance, opacity. "The object of perception constantly exceeds the limits of consciousness; the object of the image is always only the consciousness one has of it, is defined by means of this consciousness."[21] Therefore, the image of the entity, of that which is external to consciousness, is not the simulacrum or psychical representative of the entity, a sort of picture or photograph inside the mind; rather, it is the very *intending* that the specific entity x is present in the absence of x, is present insofar as the entity as external is annulled. What happens, though, if the entity that is perceived, encountered as a perceptual intention, is not really outside? If, besides not being *in* consciousness, it is also not *in* the world, but is internal-external, is itself image, not image as image-thing in the world (e.g., a painting, photograph, picture, film, digital image such as on television), but image-body that is formed in an interaction? What happens is that the difference between the intentional modality belonging to perceptual image and that belonging to mental image is attenuated, that the two intentional modes tend to merge. Such confusion appears clearly if one recalls the other two characteristics that in Sartre's view would distinguish "perception" from "image," the phenomenon of quasi-observation and spontaneity, characteristics that should constitute themselves as a result of the phenomenological investigation. Whereas perception proceeds by *Abschattungen,* the image is a synthetic act. The image is not grasped through the accumulation of adumbrations in an endless act of progressive conquest, but is given as already complete: "[I]t is organized precisely in the manner that objects are apprehended, but, in reality, it is given entirely as is, ever since its appearance."[22] The image does not keep quasi-concealed in itself an infinity of relations; rather, it is an "essential poverty." Whereas, as we have seen, the object of perception constantly exceeds the limits of consciousness, the object of the image is always only the consciousness one has of it. Now, the perception of the virtual image-body is actualized, if we want to keep this language, as image-consciousness because the percept is formed interactively as synthesis so that our knowledge of it, or the result of the interaction, emerges not from successive adumbrations of the object but from a relationally constitutive synthesis. Strangely, if purged of the theoretical weight of the reference to "consciousness," Sartre's following consideration pertains to the virtual body and not to the mental image: "The object in the image . . . does not include in itself anything more than that of which I have consciousness; conversely, however, all that is my consciousness finds its correlate in the object. . . . A paradoxical consequence ensues, namely, that the object is present to us simultaneously from the outside and from the inside. From the outside because we observe it, from the inside because it is in it that we perceive what it is."[23] With respect to the feature of "spontaneity," there too occurs, in relation to the virtual field, the process of the loss of difference that Sartre hypothesizes: "A perceptual consciousness appears to itself as passivity. In contrast, an imaginative consciousness is given to itself as imaginative consciousness, that is, as spontaneity that produces and retains the object in an image."[24] By contrast, perception of the virtual body is both passivity and activity, in which really, to use Sartrean words relative to image consciousness, "consciousness appears to itself as creative, but without positing this creative character as an object."[25] Thus, the difference between image and perception that is proposed by Sartre does not function for the virtual field. This entails that also the Sartrean idea of consciousness, which coincides with the de-realizing power of image-consciousness, is called into question.[26] What is of interest to us here, however, is the convergence that has been disclosed between the characters of image and of perception within the intentional modality that has the virtual body as its correlate. As we have seen, the analysis of dreams leads precisely to such a result.[27] One should bear in mind, however, that the virtual body is not a mental image, and we have not analyzed the structure of the mental image of the virtual body or of imagination as such, which, for our purposes, is without interest. We have simply established, by critically engaging Sartre's study of the image, that with respect to a certain region of being the image-perception difference is not an original given, and that the question as to whether the distinctive element of such image-body depends on the content of the image itself, or on the intentional modality of consciousness, is a question that cannot be answered because it involves strategies of reflection that do not work for the object under investigation. What Sartre has named *consciousness,* or the internal, or subject, as far as the virtual field is concerned, is neither point of departure nor point of arrival for the constitution of the object. Relatedly, the external as such, the world (or the external things) qua body or virtual environment, that is, in its coming to appearance, does not have a constitution that is determinate in itself.

VIRTUAL EXCESS

The virtual body is, as stated previously, interaction, a specific event that is preceded by differential structures: a body fitted with prostheses, a living synthesis of the organic and inorganic, and computer memory. The virtual body is then determined but not in the same way of the entity that we typically call "empirical object"; rather, it is determined as image, as a complex of properties perceptible by means of prostheses. Such images may or may not be recognizable; they cannot be interpreted, however, as images *of,* that is, *as* if a relationship of resemblance belonged to their nature. That is, they are not copies or simulacra except than to the extent to which, like any other entity, they maintain relations of analogy and difference. With regard to the environment-body or the virtual field, it turns out then that *even* what we call "perception" is mainly a determination or inference and not a psychic doubling. It is a determination that constitutes its object as a relational structure, rendering null the question as to which has precedence within the intentional act of constitution: whether consciousness or the object (in the language of phenomenology, whether *noesis* or *noema*). From this point of view, the virtual body exhibits in act the noetic-noematic relation;

it eventuates it, beyond any panpsychism or animation of matter by consciousness, beyond any other exteriority beside the intentional act. Simply, inside and outside, interiority and exteriority are not suitable terms for the clarification of the virtual field, although they are difficult to eliminate. Now, all this can be found in the path that takes Merleau-Ponty from the *Phenomenology of Perception* to *The Visible and the Invisible*: the virtual field, whose objects are modalities of relation, is itself a structure of correlation or relational texture of bodies understood as events of reversibility. A good descriptor of the virtual field, then, is the notion of the "flesh of the world" developed by Merleau-Ponty in his later writings, a concept that in my view resists the criticisms that many have brought against it.[28] Let us reflect on the question of the flesh[29] in order to plot a strategy in the direction of an aesthetics and an ontology of the virtual body. Husserl's well-known point of departure is as follows: insofar as it cannot be confused with other forms of knowledge, perception is a self-giving by means of adumbrations (*Abschattungen*). This means both that the thing cannot be reduced to its adumbrations and that adumbration itself is irreducible: a shadow is not destined to turn into light and the thing is, in its totality or in the full deployment of its meaning, always absent. Now, it is typical of aesthetics and its tradition to think of this structure of perception not as a defect or deficiency of the power of vision, and not even as an initial place of knowledge destined to be overcome in the distinctions of reason, but rather as an infinite power and signification that cannot be transcended. With respect to this, the issue is that of proceeding beyond Husserl, at least insofar as in Husserl in the final analysis the description of the percept remains grounded in a transcendental theory of constitution seen as relation between being-presence and universe-consciousness.[30] To my mind, the speculatively most elevated place of this aesthetic thought is to be found in Merleau-Ponty's later writings, in which he thematizes this co-belonging of *Leib* and nature in a dynamic, communicative fabric, that original element in chiasmatic explosion to which Merleau-Ponty gives the name "flesh." It is a fabric or pattern that speaks of the kinship of body and world; neither matter nor spirit, it is, rather, the expressive horizon of a "reversibility always imminent and never realized in fact."[31] Proceeding from and going beyond Husserl, Merleau-Ponty attempts to say in a new way the relation between the living body and nature [32]; he tries to think their relation in the form of an "unrefined being" or "savage" being that is the original constitution of differences, the indistinction of activity and passivity, an interweaving of perception and being perceived, the reversibility of subject and object. It is dynamic flesh, dehiscence of a being unthinkable as transcendent alterity or as common substratum beyond differences. One should not hypothesize any real stratification of experience but only the "flesh of the sensible" as a perpetual exposition of the possibilities for communication and participation. One sees in the flesh and by means of it. The flesh of the sensible is pervasive and shatters the boundary between body and world. It is the flesh of language, of history, of the idea. Now, it is easy to understand how difficult it is to express the paradoxical concept of flesh, as it means thinking an identity that is, structurally, difference without annulling itself in those differences. It is identity as process of differentiation that tries not to privilege one opposing polarity (consciousness or the thing) as the condition for the constitution of the relation.[33] One can also put the problem in this way: How does one think about the "depth" of the flesh? How does one think the relation between the visible and the invisible without recourse to the opposition of immanence and transcendence? How does one think the notion of "carnal idea"? How does one think the "immanence" of reversibility beyond any panpsychism? This is a place for the further intertwining of aesthetics and ontology. The "ontological change" proposed by Merleau-Ponty here becomes an attempt to set up a "Logos of the aesthetic world," according to Husserl's expression,[34] which does not think, however, only the active-passive expression of the living body, and thus aesthetics as a science of sensory knowledge, but which, in order to express the *Leib*-nature relation, also questions the vision-construction capacities connected to such a relation. Merleau-Ponty confers on the flesh the sense of being an "element," itself undefinable, but capable of introducing a "style of being,"

> a sort of incarnate principle that brings a style of being wherever there is a fragment of Being. The flesh is in this sense an "element" of Being. Not a fact or a sum of facts, and yet adherent to *location* and to the *now*. Much more: the inauguration of the *where* and the *when*, the possibility and exigency for the fact; in a word: facticity, what makes the fact be a fact. And, at the same time, what makes the facts have meaning, makes the fragmentary facts dispose themselves about "something."[35]

No doubt present in the flesh-element, then, is both the sense of a "house framework," the gathering of the many into one, each cohering around a nucleus that can never be intended in its purity, and the sense of a "cosmos," of that over-human opening that precedes and enables the determinacy of meaning and the possibility of the event.[36] There is no formal opposition between flesh and idea, which would be eliminativist with respect to the possibility of translating transcendence into depth, and thus reductionist in an exemplary way. Instead, in my view, the notion of flesh is effective for thinking a layer of being that precedes the organic-inorganic distinction, especially if one eliminates the subjectivist resonance that somehow marks the sense of the term, that is, if one considers carefully that "the flesh of the world is not self-feeling as is my flesh—it is sensible and non-sentient—nevertheless I call it flesh . . . in order to say that it is pregnant with possibilities."[37] It is therefore a departure from all panpsychism in the direction of the virtual. I maintain, in short, that the ontology of the flesh is a good way to think the ontology of the virtual environment, for all its peculiar characteristics. If and how it is extendible beyond this, I do not know. If we are to understand the virtual environment-world, though, we must investigate its specific conditions of possibility, first of all its space and time, in the awareness of their expression in the chiasm of bodies.[38]

5

Metaphors of the Virtual

NOTE ON SPACE

First of all virtual space, like time, or time-space if we want concretely to determine a field of experience, can be said in many ways, depending on the type of virtuality to be examined. The first movement of reflection affirms that virtual space is a field of qualitative and quantitative individuation, and thus is related to the ontology of "objects" that inhabit it. A second reflexive movement will notice that the distinction between virtual space and its objects is abstract, and thus that space should be understood as event. So, if for the sake of simplicity we assign to virtual space the value of *place of action*, then the value of action, and therefore, of place, will be relative to a typology of events. This then opens up a metaphorics of space that is particularly pervasive with regard to the virtual, almost as if the character of event-body [*corpo-evento*], in different forms and degrees, that belongs to virtual objects were to make use of the language of localization in order to institute itself, to "take up shape" or meaning. Virtual space is in this case first of all an informative, communicative, and connective space in which "proximity and distance are concepts that free themselves from their material conditions, empty themselves of their formal aspect, in order to bring out their communicative content."[1] According to McFadden, on a preliminary basis we can consider virtual pre-space or quasi-space an

> informational space with the following properties: 1) is *connected* by a network of information channels such that, if the

information is partly available to a receiver, then it is so completely, 2) there are *agents* that can change the information and well-known *protocols* for exchanging information between them. This is the "consensual" part of the original definition. Agents can also be part of the information space and thus be subject to change.[2]

Such a pre-virtual space, which can be exemplified by computer networks, is for Pierre Lévy the space of cyberculture, "the communication space made accessible through the global interconnection of computers and computer memories,"[3] a visualized form of information streams (in which it can be said with characteristic approximation that "the objects . . . are neither physical objects, nor, necessarily, representations of objects, but rather in form and substance, constructed of data, of pure information"),[4] or "spatialized visualization of information in global systems of information processing,"[5] which allows actions of control, collection, data exploration, and intercommunication among users. An analysis of these virtual quasi-spaces, that is, an analysis that reflects the specificity of technologies and their uses, is clearly of interest at different levels—psychological, anthropological, sociological—at least because as inhabited, above all emotionally, space is transformed into place (the spatiality and temporality of e-mail, forums, chat, hypertext, Web, are different as well as similar, and produce peculiar perceptual, emotional, and cognitive situations).[6] This is not a question that I can consider here, but it is worth mentioning that these spatialities can be understood in a generically "cultural" way:

> Semantic, metaphorical space . . . is that in which cyberculture takes shape and is nourished and developed, in which the physical body has a role as symbolic, virtual image . . . The immediacy and universality of a communication that is proposed as a process of "deterritorialization," of the loss of boundaries, of the possibility of living in cyberspace, of the power to go "beyond the sense of place."[7]

This improper level of spatiality has actually given origin to a problem that is quite interesting from the theoretical point of view.

SIDE REMARKS: THE COMMUNITY

Thanks, in fact, to the spread of computer networks, a new idea of community has been established, defined by its theorists as "virtual community," "collective intelligence,"[8] or "global brain."[9] It is a type of community that turns its being ephemeral and open into its fundamental element. A descriptive approach will have to become aware of the types of community that have really been established online, of how communication functions in them in relation to the new possibilities offered by the medium, and so forth. From the theoretical point of view, though, the new models of community imply a coherent redefinition of the very concepts of individual and community. These issues, of which I here offer only a sketch, are relevant and complex.[10] The individual of the virtual community is an individual in name only. In the electronic community, it is the linguistic definition of the role that constitutes a being-this, that is, that identifies the individual, thereby allowing membership. It is the case of a "linguistic" individual whose propensities and capacities are not mediated or integrated by language, but are, rather, dissolved in the language that he or she adopts. One can say, perhaps, that the individual of a virtual community is exemplary, that is, is an example, insofar as exemplary is only the purely linguistic, that is, that which is not defined by any property other than its being *said* or being said *as*. In examples, *being said* is the property that grounds possible memberships; that is, it is the property that establishes the common being of individualities, or that enables a community. It is a purely linguistic community, one which gives itself only within a space of communication that is not grounded, in principle, on actual membership. We thus catch a glimpse of the possibility of inessential communities,[11] that is, communities in which the gathering in no way concerns an essence (this being a determination or function that allows for a more than merely nominal definition), or communities present solely within the space of communication, which obviously take on as much force and meaning as the technological, social, and political spaces permit. In short, in the virtual community there appears a strong and inaugural sense of speech, which transforms individuals into members of a class whose only boundaries are the linguistic properties common to its members. Paradoxically, an absolute nominalism is turned upside-down into an absolute realism. It is perhaps Jean-Luc Nancy[12] who has made the most conspicuous effort to think the inessential community, building a model that could be exemplified by virtual communities. According to Nancy, the radically finite being of humans can be expressed in the formula, "existence is without essence": the human being, as much as any other being in existence, is in itself "en route," transitive, that is, radically "exposed":

> "Being-self" is being-unto-itself, being-exposed-to-itself; but "*soi*" in itself *is nothing but the exposition*. Being-unto-itself is being-unto-exposition. It is being-unto-others, if "others" declines "in itself and for itself" the declension of "*soi*." All ontology can be reduced to this being-unto-self-unto-others. Transitively, essence *is* nothing more than the exposition of its subsistence. . . . This is what we will transcribe by saying that there is no communion, there is no common being, but there is being *in* common. Once ontology becomes this logic of being in itself as being *to* itself, all ontology can be reduced to the in-common of the *unto*-itself.[13]

In other words, there is not a "subject" that enters into relations with others, but a singularity that "co-appears," and co-appears only in the community. Nor is there a common being to be achieved through work, for example, the work of politics, but rather a community that is more originary than the individual, and therefore than the social relationships that the individual establishes. Community is present when singularities expose themselves and, while remaining as singular, they share their exposition. This is a "logic of limit," writes Nancy, "a logic of what does not belong to the pure inside or outside,"[14] a logic that characterizes the being-with, which is situated "between the disintegration of the 'crowd,' and the aggregation of the 'group,' and both are in every possible moment virtual, forthcoming: this suspension characterizes the 'being-with': a relationship without relationship, a simultaneous exposure to relationship and the absence of relationship."[15] In brief, Nancy strives to subtract the idea of community from that of a substantial common being that would be realized through political work. Instead, he thinks of community as an original given, more originary than any other social, economic, or political bond; he thinks of it, that is, as a "compearance," an *appearing together* that mutually commits us to one another while at the same time maintaining us as singularities that share their very own division.[16] One therefore always experiences community as a limit, as that which represents a risk to the social bond. This is precisely what seems to happen to the communities that exist as language in that hypertext elevated to power that is precisely the computer network. As is well known, according to some theorists this opens up new possibilities. Lévy foresees a new anthropological space, a space of knowledge different from the medial space of commodities:

> Within the space of reproduction, distribution, and indefinite variation, signs no longer convoke the things they designate, nor the beings that announce them. . . . Not only does the sign no longer refer to an absent object, it can no longer lead us back to the start of the series, to the "original," since, within the commodity space, the sign is merely the byproduct of the processes of recording, reproduction, and distribution. It is only a sign within the circuit of transmission.

On the contrary, "the space of knowledge" permitted by computer networks

> is defined by the return of being, of real and living existence within the sphere of signification. . . . Within the knowledge space, collective intellects reconstruct a plane of immanence of signification in which beings, signs, and things exist in a dynamic relationship of mutual participation.[17]

The issue here is not to assess the theoretical and practical conditions for the possibility of the actualization and exercise of this "space" or place of collective intelligence, but rather to find ways of integration among apparently very different memories and forms of subjectivity and community.[18] With respect to this task, an aesthetics of the virtual is only a propaedeutic work. We can note, however, that reflection on the concept of community as being-with, or limit-community, has led to a result that is essential for our thinking about the virtual field in the strict sense. This result consists in the priority of relation as opposed to subjectivity:

The *in* (the *with*, the Latin *cum* of "community") does not designate any mode of the relation. It would designate rather a being *insofar as it is* relation, identical to existence itself—that is, identical to the arrival of existence, to existence.[19]

This is a point to which we will have to return.

Having concluded these side remarks, let us now proceed. So far, we have considered virtual quasi-space or pre-space, and have quickly pointed to its cultural dimension. In order to delineate the conceptual boundaries of virtual space, at least in its dimension as a space of information, we can add to the properties of connection and interaction the characteristic of immersivity. The task then is to see what this means. We still follow McFadden:

> 3. There are *agents* that can transform, abstract, and represent the information in the cyberspace so that a human can experience it as humans experience the space and "everyday" objects of the world. Humans may be "in" cyberspace as they are in space. This is the "delusional" part of the original definition.[20]

In order not to lose its specificity, however, we cannot think of virtual space as mere simulation of space. McFadden's reference to *agents* duly shifts our attention to the concept of virtual space as a space of action, an active space, a space of events, which, as informational, is a cultural product.[21] [Such a product], however, is not simply "external" or other than the mind-body that perceives and interprets it, is not an alterity comprehensible by means of perceptual and mental operations. Rather, it is an internal-external product insofar as it is constituted by interaction and inhabited through the interaction (I do not believe, as is often claimed, that such a space is currently actualized in computer networks, even though it may become an extroflection of them in the future insofar as there do not seem to be theoretical motivations why [Internet] sites may not structure themselves as virtual spaces). In this regard, Queau has brought attention to two interesting elements: in his view, virtual space is

> a database of interactive graphics that can be explored and visualized in real time in the form of three-dimensional computer-

generated images to give the feeling of immersion into the image. In more complex forms, the virtual environment is an authentic "synthetic space" in which one can experience the sensation of being able to move "physically."[22]

Hence, despite the ambiguity of the term *image,* there emerge two directions of study: the architecture of the "space of synthesis" and the immersion *into* image, or "the intimate hybridization between the body of the spectator-actor and the space in which he is immersed."[23] In following the first direction, we will have to address themes related to a physics of the processes of virtual space. In following the second, our research will be oriented toward a psychology of processes. With regard to a physics of discrete spatiality, the productive, organizational, and therefore architectonic modalities of virtual space sometimes but not always begin with the destruction of continuous space and then proceed, from its translation into information units, to its reorganization in a perceptible environment. With regard to architecture, at least for a still nonspecific level of virtual space, it can be remarked that

> a sequence of bits, initially without form, receives form from a schema of representation, and information emerges from the interaction of data with the representation: diverse representations allow one to highlight different relationships within the same body of data. The mode of appearing is a subsequent effect caused by many layers of patterns that act on other schemes, some as data, others as code.[24]

If we temporarily bracket the polyvocal term *representation,* we see that in virtual space the standard interface should be user-configurable through his or her actions. Users thus take part in the constitution of space by means of their load of habits, expectations, emotions, memory, and information, and they literally *give place* to a space-environment that may not be, or may be not only, "embodied fantasy, constructed on a fundamental representation of our imagination,"[25] but is certainly a place of relation. Therefore:

> The case of cyberspace shows clearly how what we call the spatialization of information is not (or is not always and

necessarily) the result of the acquisition of external information, but constitutes, in this case, the product of the confluence of the latter and internal information.[26]

PERCEPTUAL INTERACTION

We shall have to return later to the general significance of this relational structure; for now, we will stress that the structure emerges from virtual space primarily as perceptual space,[27] that is, according to the other direction of inquiry opened up by the notions of interactivity and immersivity. I wish here to limit my considerations to visual perception, whereas I am not certain that we can apply the Gibsonian idea of an environmental optic array to the description of an interactive space because such an array describes rules of invariance that show the permanence of the relations[28] connecting homogeneous areas of the optic array; but perhaps one can describe such rules of invariance only if one supposes the existence of objects that, although certainly subject to change, nevertheless have a structure stable in itself. Conversely, I find Arnheim's theory of visual perception[29] to be persuasive as far as it approaches a description of interaction:

> If in every visual experience shape, color, and movement possess dynamic qualities, we must ask more explicitly: how does the dynamics get into the percept?. . . . The stimulus material reaching our eyes acquires dynamics while it is being processed by the nervous system. . . . Perception reflects an invasion of the organism by external forces, which upset the balance of the nervous system. A hole is torn in a resistant tissue. . . . At no time does stimulation congeal into a static arrangement.[30]

Now, one could argue that in the virtual field there occurs a synergistic action through which "a hole is torn in [the] resistant tissue" of the virtual body, as well as in the prostheticized body of the user. Moreover, the structure of the perceived reflects an invasion on the part of *relatively* external forces and is configured qua phenomenon or as a horizon of expressive qualities by the latter. It is clear that the dynamic structure of the virtual field is different from the fields important to Arnheim's work, which in the first place has taught us to take into account the specific value of the medium. But it seems to me that some relevant places in Arnheim's theory of visual perception may just serve in our understanding of the shape of the virtual field as a field of interactive perceptions. Regarding the theme of shape, we find in Arnheim what is essential:

> The physicists' description of the optical process is well known. . . . But what about the corresponding psychological experience? . . . the world of images does not simply imprint itself upon a faithfully sensitive organ. Rather, in looking at an object, we reach out for it. With an invisible finger we move through the space around us, go out to the distant places where things are found, touch them, catch them, scan their surfaces, trace their borders, explore their texture. Perceiving shapes is an eminently active occupation.[31]

This clear and persuasive description of the psychological experience corresponding to perceptual activity (his description of the haptic character of vision has a Merleau-Pontian flavor) is in virtual space descriptive of the relation to the virtual body. Also in Arnheim, of course within the limits of a theory of *visual* perception is the key to understanding the conditions of possibility of interactive perception. It is clear that for Arnheim, vision does not proceed simply from the particular to the general—as it is structural shapes that make up the primary data—and therefore he does not accept an empiricist relation between sensory data and representation (or better, mental *image*). Precisely because structural shapes are the *primary data* of perception, it is also clear that, on the one hand, emphasizing the aspect of *data* will prevent an absolute constructivism, and on the other, emphasizing the *primacy* of data will cut off the abstractive process, which, from percept, leads to the universal via species of sensible and intelligible order. On the one hand, this theory is useful for the development of virtual environments insofar as it implies that the simulation of perceptual qualities may be articulated not on the basis of precise similarities, but rather on the basis of the preeminent characteristics that allow identification and can make the object appear as "a complete, integrated pattern."[32] Especially relevant and fruitful, however, is, on the other hand, the issue that is thus raised, namely, that of the explicit absence of any particular stimulus pattern:

> The new theory poses a particular problem. The overall structural features of which the percept is thought to consist are obviously not furnished explicitly by any particular stimulus pattern. . . . [T]he stimulus configuration enters the perceptual process only in the sense that it awakens in the brain a specific pattern of general sensory categories. This pattern "stands for" the stimulation . . . percepts cannot contain the stimulus material "itself," either totally or partially.[33]

Arnheim thus presents the problem of the spontaneity of perception, that is, of the constitution of a formal scheme. He uses, as we know, the expression "perceptual concepts"; by this, however, he does not mean to interpret perception as an intellectual act, but rather to show an analogy. In perception, operations are present that a certain tradition has considered as belonging to thought; therefore, perception as a whole, but also in its differential features, can be understood as an *analogon rationis* [an analogue of reason], in line with the tradition of modern aesthetics that has been inaugurated by Baumgarten and that, with accents and modalities and through different pathways, has been accepted by both phenomenology and hermeneutics in the twentieth century. To suppose that shape is the primary given of perception and at the same time that it is not provided explicitly by a particular stimulus pattern allows many implications that concern the virtual. In the first place, it can be adapted to the virtual as a theory of interaction: "Perceptual shape is the outcome of an interplay between the physical object, the medium of light acting as the transmitter of information, and the conditions prevailing in the nervous system of the viewer."[34] If the *physical* object (understood in any sense of the term *physical*) is not the "perceptual shape," then it is possible to interpret the object as a result of interaction, and we have, with good approximation, a relevant trait of a theory of perception in the virtual field. It is clear that we cannot simply export Arnheim's theory of perception to the virtual field, but we are on the right path. If, for example, as Arnheim explicitly admits, we include within the "nervous system of the viewer" the influence of past perception, and we think of that past in the broad sense of a memory that contributes to shape, then we acquire another element of the theory. Indeed, concerning the *influence* of the past on the configuration of the percept Arnheim remarks:

Every visual experience is embedded in a context of space and time. Just as the appearance of objects is influenced by that of neighboring objects in space, so also is it influenced by sights that preceded it in time. But to acknowledge these influences is not to say that everything surrounding an object automatically modifies its shape and color or, to pursue the argument to its extreme, that the appearance of an object is merely the product of all the influences exerted upon it.[35]

Now, a virtual body is certainly not *automatically* modified by what surrounds it; yet it is a body that just is—in terms of its appearance—the user's perceptions, which are always spatiotemporal, at least in the sense of being both perceptions of events (and in fact the virtual body is peculiarly an event-object [*oggetto-evento*]) and, insofar as the virtual body is concerned, a meeting between memories, namely, a global memory or a memory that corresponds to the possibilities of interpretation and action of the user's mind-body, and a computer memory, a model of language structured at multiple levels. Obviously, at the origin of computer memory there is another, or more than one, global memory, with its technological knowledge and determinate informational intentions. The field of interaction, or virtual environment, is then rendered effective by hardware implementation, whose specificities outline the limits of possibility for the interaction and thus also for the modification of the virtual body. So, not even in a virtual environment is "what we see . . . determined entirely by what we have seen before."[36] In the virtual environment, rather, it becomes clearer "that memory traces of familiar objects may influence the shape we perceive."[37] In fact, a theory of perception in virtual environments concerns events, since the virtual body is an event-object [*oggetto-evento*], and this implies a reflection on time that we will have to attempt. In the meantime, however, Arnheim has allowed us to focus our attention on what is essential: the explicit *absence* of a particular stimulus pattern, which is the turning point between a merely recording conception of perception and a conception that is also constitutive of it. This also enables us to interpret [perception] as both exploration and constitution, as an activity that is an interweaving of activity and passivity—poles that can be separated only at the level of abstract analysis. This leads—if one were to inquire into the relation between configuration and form—to remarkable consequences regarding the identity of the perceived object ("the identity of a visual object depends . . . not so much on its shape as such as on the structural skeleton created by the shape")[38] and, correspondingly, the identity of the constructed object, in a way that cuts to the root of any banally mimetic or "illusionistic" conception, whether artistic or not, of the image. It may therefore be of some interest to underscore that this absence, emptiness, lack, signaled by Arnheim, opens up a dimension that escapes computation.[39] For Arnheim, visual concepts, which are derivates of perceptual experience, are not to be confused with eidetic images, "physiological vestiges of direct stimulation."[40] Now, the condition of possibility of the *difference* between cognitive and computational processes consists precisely in the giving of an absence, in the opening of a lack, in the presence of a place of interruption within a continuous process. But unlike, for example, Sartre's view, which in the imagination grasps a moment of nullification that speaks of the constitution of consciousness as freedom, Arnheim accents the constitutive aspect made possible by lack. Without confusing perceptual concepts with representational concepts, without circuiting processes with products, Arnheim highlights their gradual differentiation because perception itself is an active exploration that grasps forms.[41] This entails a thematization of the expressive dynamic, that is, the perceptual and interpretive dynamic that goes beyond the horizon of propositional representations in the direction of symbolic expression. It is not of interest here to develop this theme, which goes in the direction of the intertwined notions of art and symbolism. It is, however, important to note, for an aesthetics of the virtual, that expressive qualities are a dynamic aspect of perception, and that their meaning cannot be grasped by making perceptual activity static or by dividing it into parts. Expressive qualities are for Arnheim the primary and proper object of perception; they are the psychological correlate of tensions that are activated at the neurophysiological and, more generally, biological level in order to organize phenomena and generate perceptual concepts; they appears as a play of forces that intrinsically galvanize forms and dimensions and whose representation is, so to speak, a metaphor for mental forces. Grasped in this respect, the visual pattern will be always inflected toward the future, will always be irreducible to a dialectic of static (subject-object, internal-external) and preestablished polarities, and will instead be thinkable as a qualitative-expressive sense that is constituted in the interaction.

From this point of view, the difference indicated by Arnheim between adjectival and adverbial qualities[42] is relevant for an aesthetics of the virtual, because it implies that aesthetic qualities, as adverbial, have to do with verb modes, that is, actions, which in the case of perception is an interaction. Aesthetic qualities are not really the *content* of experience, as resulting from a passive synthesis, but belong rather to the interactive, temporal, event-related, and effectual dynamic. Now, this dynamic, which is the qualitative genesis or origin of meaning, is *constitutive* of the virtual field. If we were to apply the idea of expressive adverbial property to what we generally call the "art world" and to so-called artistic productions, an operation carried out by Arnheim especially with respect to the visual arts, we would notice the significant explanatory power [of such an idea], most considerably if we were to augment, so to speak, the level of our attention to historical density or to the cultural layers that affect expressive qualities. The idea seems to me very useful, though, for understanding the endeavors of interactive art, endeavors which, although perhaps not yet proper examples of virtual art, nevertheless stretch the possibilities of production techniques to their limit and in the direction of virtual art.[43] In other words, for its specificity and with respect to the idea of adverbial qualities, the virtual medium seems to be an optimal field in which to apply the theory, at least insofar as the history of interactive installations has gradually moved from interaction in terms of sensorial participation to participation mediated by a pervasive but transparent interface, for which the machine becomes an organ of participation for the spectators, transforming them into spectators-actors. At the level of works on visibility, one should bear in mind by way of example the installation by Christa Sommerer and Laurent Mignonneu, "HAZE Express" (1999), in which the visitor changes and redesigns the quality of the landscape as visible from a train window by touching the surface, or "Anamorphose numérique" (2002) by Miguel Almiron,[44] or the installation by Studio Azzurro "Mediterranean Meditations" (2003). Such works attempt to place the viewer in the intermediary zone of the interface that enables an action capable of causing qualitatively and therefore perceptually complex changes. In these experiments, the work-environment [*ambiente-opera*] is shaped, in fact, as an interface-environment [*ambiente-interfaccia*], rather than as a world-environment [*ambiente-mondo*]: "One can define the interface as a machine: a functional device, operative without waste, without noise. An interface as transparent space, as circular space, space of circulation, a space in which there are no objects, but only flowing currents."[45]

In the virtual world-environment, that is, an environment that is not just interactive but is, rather, constituted out of interaction, it is the body that carries out the role of interface, that constitutes the relational history of the environment.[46] It is, however, an environment that results from the integration of the natural and the artificial, human being and machine, "a pairing that generates an intense synergy and new nature, otherwise inconceivable . . . the limpid and clear world of the algorithm, and the organic and psychical world of sensations and gestures . . . intersect through the porous *paroi* of the interface."[47]

A NOTE ON TIME

Arnheim's conception of expressive adverbial properties, however, opens up various perspectives: it almost naturally implies the development of a philosophy of expression that could provide a conceptual framework such as to enable, within the specificity of the virtual environment-body [*corpo-ambiente*], the inflection of classical aesthetic categories such as mimesis, representation, and image. In my view, the philosophies that have thought the category of expression most deeply in terms of its being both a structural principle and a principle of comprehension of reality are those of Spinoza and Leibniz, which constitute a mutual alternative.[48] One could just recall the fact that for Spinoza the event or singular thing, which is identity of body and idea and at the same time of bodily affection and mental image, is the certain and determined *expression* of the free power of nature, that is, of the attributes of substance, and that for Leibniz the monad is a universe-world concentrated in an expressive point of view or perspective that is the whole world. While it is certainly not our task here to explain these powerful models[49] (although we shall return later to Leibniz in relation to a specific point involving the virtual), I simply want to point out that Wunenburger very appropriately finds in these philosophies the place from which the idea of "expressive image emerged."[50] What is most important now is that the expressive qualities are a *dynamic* aspect of perception whose meaning cannot be grasped by rendering perceptual activity static or by dividing it into parts. So, from the point of view of a psychology of perception that aims at investigating the virtual field, it will be relevant to study changes in quality. This means, more generally, that a theory of the perception of virtual bodies will have to take time into account, or at least consider that a geometry of time-space is never given a priori and the constitution of the field requires that attention be paid to the peculiarities of its matter. This leads, on the one hand, to a deeper exploration of the ontology of the virtual body, and on the other, because of the event-related nature of virtual objects, to the study of the perception of events (which has some illustrious historical precedents). To be sure, it is not easy to establish the notion of event and the correlated conception of time, and the very idea of a "psychic presence-time" is problematic. It is, however, a relevant program in general, perhaps not only because there are "cases in which the fact of perception is achieved solely on the ground of a temporally extended content of consciousness,"[51] but also because, radically, there are no cases where this does not occur. This is clearly not only a problem of measurement, as it is not easy and perhaps not even possible to match physical time[52] (however one wants to define it, assuming it could be measured) and psychological time.[53] If one's understanding of the virtual is in terms of an event-object [*oggetto-evento*] and is as such a dynamic understanding of time,[54] or, in other words, if the virtual image-object [*oggetto-immagine*] is not thinkable as static or as simply present (because it is interactive), then one will need to examine the question of time in greater detail. If we position ourselves from the point of view of a psychology of perception, it is possible to affirm that even objects are events, and to establish a table of correspondence between constancy of stimulus and type of perception. From this point of view, what we perceive as "objects" will be relatively stationary events or, if you will, "happenings"; non-stationary events will be related to a variable stimulus and will be perceivable as movements and qualitative changes. In this way, physical descriptions of the relative variation and constancy of the stimulation (for example, locally variable in space, constant during phases but not between phases, a variation that remains below the threshold of perception of movement and qualitative change) may be matched by phenomenal descriptions of quasi-stationary or quasi-continuous events or pseudo-events.[55] All this, however, is not sufficient because the stimulus-percept relation is not, so to speak, a relation of linear causality, since the effect is not *virtually* present in the cause, and a direct translation from physical time to phenomenological time is problematic. Furthermore, it is clearly necessary to examine the problem of event as a problem of object-time relation, or, to use traditional terms, of entity-becoming.

Now, in order to demonstrate quickly the aporias entailed in the concept of time-present [*tempo-presente*] so as to articulate the temporality of the virtual event-body [*corpo-evento*], let us move at once to a high level of reflection, taking as our example Derrida's analysis in "*Ousia* and *Gramme*." As is well known, Derrida questions an important note in *Being and Time* wherein Heidegger inspects the "vulgar concept" of time as established by Aristotle.[56] The question is justified by the need to address the problem of "time" in view of a destruction of traditional ontology: the essential link between being and time is internal to the notions, originally temporal, of present, presence, *parousia*, *ousia*. The situation produced is circular: a certain semanticization of the concept of time implies a sense of being as *parousia*, and at the same time the whole concept of *parousia* involves a particular reading of the phenomenon of "time." To this end, Derrida writes: "From Parmenides to Husserl, the privilege of the present has never been put into question. It could not have been. It is what is self-evident itself, and no thought seems possible outside its element."[57] Thus, both past and future are and must be thought of in the form of presence: as past present or future present. Heidegger *seems* to move against this. Obviously, Derrida's adopted strategy to read Heidegger's criticism of Aristotle is complex, as it slides continuously in an interweaving of texts of Kant, Hegel, and Bergson. Moreover, such a strategy opens up serious theoretical problems that are often purposely marginalized in the notes. All of this will have to be left in the background, however, as what is of interest here is to note Derrida's progressively increasing concentration on concepts of number (as what is numbered and that which numbers) and *grammé*. Primarily in relation to Aristotle's position, this concentration brings out a sense of the structure of the now (*nun*) that I would call *ontological differential*:

> Not to be able to coexist with an other (the same as itself), with an other now, is not a predicate of the now, but its essence as presence. The now, presence in the act of the present, is constituted as the impossibility of coexisting with an other now, that is, with an other-the-same-as-itself. The now *is* (in the present indicative) the impossibility of coexisting *with*

itself. With itself, that is, with an other self, an other now, an other same, a double.⁵⁸

Such impossibility is disclosed, though, as the possibility of the impossible:

> The impossible—the coexistence of two nows—appears only in a synthesis—taking this world neutrally, implying no position, no activity, no agent—let us say in a certain complicity or coimplication *maintaining* together several current nows [*maintenants*] which are said to be the one past and the other future. . . . Time is a name for this impossible possibility.⁵⁹

Leaving unnoticed, then, the problem of numbering, or of the operator of the synthesis, which, for Aristotle, is the problem of the possible character of the soul's ontological determinacy with respect to time, Derrida's discourse emphasizes the necessity of the connection between the coimplication of the now and the spatiotemporal complex. Space as possible coexistence (the coimplication that *holds together*) becomes, as temporalized, a space of impossible coexistence. In other words, time can only be thought of in connection with space, but space loses its sense of possible coexistence if thought in connection with time, since it is impossible for two nows to coexist. On the other hand, it is impossible to think not only time without space, but also space without time. In Aristotle, as we know, the spatiotemporal nexus is exhibited in the word *hama*:

> In Greek *hama* means "together," "all at once," both together, "at the same time." This locution is first neither spatial nor temporal. . . . It says complicity, the common origin of time and space, appearing together [*com-paraitre*] as the condition for all appearing of Being. In a certain way it says the dyad as the minimum.⁶⁰

The word *hama,* then, a sign of the necessary though impossible possibility of connecting space and time, describes an *aporia*: the tendency to think the now as a point, albeit in the knowledge that "the now is not the point, since it does not arrest time, is neither time's origin, end, or limit. At least it is not a limit *to the extent that* it belongs to time."[61] So the now must and at the same time cannot be thought of as a point. It therefore cannot be thought of as a *part* in act, that is, as a point on a line that is *itself* actual [*in atto*], and likewise, time cannot be thought of as a *series* of points on a line. This does not preclude, however, our retention of the *gramme* [line] analogy, as time continues to be thought of as an actual line: the now as an always inactual point can and must be thought—and therefore present itself, be present—as that which in essence belongs to *grammé*. In other words, if it is not possible to think of time as analogous to a *certain* (I would say, abstract) *structure* of the *gramme* (understood as a series of parts-points), this does not mean that it is not necessary to maintain the analogy between time and *gramme* if time is considered not "as a series of potential limits, but as a line in act, as a line thought on the basis of its extremities (*ta eskhata*)."[62] A line completed and actual (and therefore present to thought) constitutes the condition of possibility of time, of inscribing time into thought. Therefore:

> *Time*, then, would be but the name of the limits within which the *gramme* is thus comprehended, and, along with the *gramme*, the possibility of the trace in general. *Nothing* other *has ever been* thought by the name of *time*. Time is that which is thought on the basis of Being as presence, and if something—which bears a relation to time, but is not time—is to be thought beyond the determination of Being as presence, it cannot be a question of something that still could be called *time*.[63]

Opened up before us, then, is the theme or problem of the impossibility of escaping from that line that is thought in act and that constitutes dynamics in terms of teleology, that is, as the ordered tension of an incomplete that can be obviously considered as such only within the horizon, or in view, of that which is complete. Grammatically, the line closes on itself, becomes a circle. Leaving the circle is impossible because a contrary or inverted way of thinking is internal to the very potentiality of metaphysical thought, which can sustain it, can not only bear [*sopportarlo*] but also support it [*supportarlo*], within a game of submission and subtraction "belonging as much to the de-limitation of metaphysics as the thought of the present, as to the simple overturning of metaphysics."⁶⁴ Whether the now is understood as partly constitutive of time or as accidental and extraneous, it is important to keep in mind, and we shall have to return to this in our effort to grasp the virtual, that, in any event,

> the enigma of the now is dominated in the difference between act and potentiality. . . . *On the other hand*, time, as the number of movement, is on the side of non-Being, matter potentiality, incompletion. Being in act, energy, is not time, but eternal presence. . . . But, *on the other hand*, time is not non-Being, and non-Beings are not in time. In order to be in time, something must have begun to be and to tend, like every potentiality, toward act and form.⁶⁵

What remains (the rest) is the conception of *ousia* as *parousia*. In conclusion: there is not, contrary to Heidegger's view, a "vulgar concept of time," that is, a "metaphysical" concept of time that could be countered with an alternative view. *Another* concept of time does not exist: "[I]n attempting to produce this *other* concept, one rapidly would come to see that it is constructed out of other metaphysical or ontotheological predicates."⁶⁶ "Time," then, belongs to metaphysical conceptuality.

Reflecting on time (which, it turns out, is also the problem of space or place) therefore implies walking at the border of such conceptuality. The impossibility of traversing this border toward a space-time of the origin, of the beginning, of the authentic has been repeatedly denounced. In the final analysis, however, this is an attempt at the philosophical management of a residue of nihilism. It is certainly true that "now x is not x." This is so not because time as the number of becoming presupposes a multiplicity of isolated, independent unities, different "nows" that are cut and separated from the whole and thus rendered undifferentiated; rather, this is so because the now is always the experience of an appearing (or, the appearing of experience; in another language we would say that it is the opening of a world, or rather, the place in which the world-opening difference becomes event), and this unity of experience, that is, the positive that is the appearing of an entity, becomes nothingness. So, precisely because the now cannot be understood only abstractly as an entity-point, of the entity that exists as the now one must by necessity predicate nothingness. Now, can this simple and banal sense of temporal becoming produce any meaning?⁶⁷

Here, the discussion can open up once again in the direction of the virtual. In fact, the thinking that coherently reaches the at least apparently aporetic situation described above thinks of relations as of encounters *between* entities capable of development, or as actualizations of a potentiality that is present in actual entities as their guiding principle. One must clarify, then, if the virtual follows the same logic. The metaphor of the "passing" of time, or if one prefers, the experience of becoming, involves the presentation of novelty: it speaks of a nonrepetition that implies *at the same time* both absolute and relative novelty. Such is expressed in the dialectic of potentiality and actuality. According to it, becoming is the act of an entity in potency insofar as it is potential, and therefore novelty, which too is experience of what has not yet been, is relative to that which the act makes possible. Now, potentiality and actuality are co-principles of the entity (any entity). This implies both that novelty (the future) does not originate from nothingness and that it does not emerge from something other than or from the exterior to, so to speak, the entity in becoming: the process of becoming changes the entity intrinsically and is not to be confused with an either simple or complicated movement of addition or subtraction of parts. What occurs, then, is a novelty of being that has its reason for being in the entity in actuality, which possesses such novelty in potency, that is, intrinsically, authentically, insofar as potentiality is a principle of the entity. In this process, potentiality does not become actuality, because in that case one would have an infinite reduplication of the potentiality-actuality relation. Rather, it is the entity that actualizes potentiality, or that expresses its own potentialities. Potentiality and actuality are not entities in a reciprocal, intrinsic, and necessary relation; rather, they are principles of the entity that are really distinct, so that their ontological consistency is their relation. They are, therefore, transcendental relations: actuality is a determining and determined principle, whereas potentiality is a determinable and undetermined principle. It should be noticed that I have not made any reference to the concepts of substance and accident, or of matter and form, or of final and efficient causes. Nor have I distinguished between active potentiality and passive potentiality, or between *causa essendi* [cause of being] and *causa fiendi* [cause of becoming], and therefore I have not maintained that the entity is identifiable as something other than its becoming, or as having permanence as opposed to becoming.[68] It does not matter that the ontological position is phenomenalist rather than substantalist, idealistic rather than empiricist. I simply wonder whether one can think of the entity as an event without thinking of the potentiality-actuality relation. I believe the answer is no, unless one renounces the sense of time, becoming, novelty that involves both construction and dissolution, and one maintains that everything is eternal. The virtual, however, compels us to think this relation in a certain way, a way, to be sure, that configures its own field but that can also have interesting consequences. To understand this, we must explore the concept of the virtual more deeply.

6

The Concept of the Virtual

We have already alluded to the development of the concept of the virtual by Lévy. Let us follow the question more closely. Lévy writes:

> The word "virtual" is derived from the Medieval Latin *virtualis*, itself derived from *virtus*, meaning strength or power. In scholastic philosophy the virtual is that which has potential rather than actual existence. The virtual *tends* toward actualization, without undergoing any form of effective or formal concretization. . . . Strictly speaking, the virtual should not be compared with the real but the actual, for virtuality and actuality are merely two different ways of being.[1]

I do not find the *motif* of "contraposition" to be persuasive, but the consequences are interesting:

> In one sense the entity conveys and produces its virtualities. An event, for example, reorganizes a previous problematic and is susceptible of being interpreted in various ways. In another sense the virtual constitutes the entity. The virtualities inherent in a being, its problematic, the knot of tensions, constraints, and projects that animates it, the questions that move it forward, are an essential element of its determination.[2]

At this point, however, Lévy plays the virtual-actual pair against the possible-real pair, where the sense of the opposition between possible and virtual is taken from Deleuze. This is a delicate point, and we must understand what, for Deleuze, constitutes the sense of the opposition. Lévy, in any case, makes use of it as follows: "The possible is already fully constituted, but exists in a state of limbo. It can be realized without any change occurring either in its determination or nature. It is a phantom reality, something latent. The possible is exactly like the real, the only thing missing being existence."[3]

So the possible is stillness, inactivity, whereas the virtual is a node of tendencies or a dynamic-problematic complex. This allows Lévy to construct an "ontological square" that intersects possible and real, virtual and actual, with moments of latency and manifestations of substances and events. Within it, the actual and the virtual articulate the event as a not predefined process, as a nexus of attempts to respond (actualization) to problematic complexes (virtualization), or as "being as creation," whereas the process of realization is a selection of definite possibilities in which the possible is also thought of as "a *form* upon which realization confers a *material* embodiment."[4] A sphere of latency that comprises both the insistence of the possible and the existence of the virtual is the condition for a field of manifestation in which the real subsists and the actual happens. The possible and the real are in turn modes of being of substance and constitute its dialectics. The virtual and the actual are modes of the being and dialectic of the event, as mentioned before. As we already know,[5] for Lévy "the real, substance, the thing, *subsists*"; the possible harbors nonmanifest forms that *insist* in the real; the virtual, whose essence consists in an exit, *exists*; and the actual, which is the manifestation of an event, *happens*.[6] Lévy's proposal, which is further complicated by the endeavor to interpret the modes of being or processes in accord with a causal scheme (realization as material cause, potentialization—one should say *possibilization*—as formal cause, both belonging to the order of selection; actualization as efficient cause, and virtualization as final cause, both understood as creative processes), has several interesting points: namely, the concept of the virtual as a problematic, dynamic node, and the conception of the path *from* virtual *to* actual, which means that virtualization ought to be thought of as a process at the same time internal and external to the happening, to the self-actualization of the event. It is internal as a "problem," as "nodes of constraint," and therefore as "ends that inspire acts." It is external with respect to a reproductive dynamic, and such that it can constitute a condition of novelty (thanks to which "actualization invents a solution to the problem posed by the virtual. In so doing . . . it *invents a form*, creates a radically new information").[7] One should also take into consideration that Lévy sharply reinterprets as virtualization complex processes that emerge in the economic, the social, and so on, and that he is not therefore primarily interested in the concept of the virtual as derived from an analysis of the virtual body. The concept of the virtual is rather a "way" of being, which together with those of the real, the possible, the present, functions as a descriptor of the complex of entities and their processes: "Real, possible, actual, and virtual are four different ways of being, but almost always act together in every concrete phenomenon that can be analyzed."[8] Finally, the virtual-possible opposition too can be thought, according to Lévy, as a function whose terms can be exchanged and reconfigured in process. We are not here interested in elaborating a general ontology by which to interpret the virtual moment in "every analyzable concrete situation." It should be made clear, however, that the virtual-possible opposition in the terms proposed by Lévy makes no sense ontologically and leads to a substance-event dualism whose effects even Lévy strives to reduce. His is the strange conception of the possible as something (an entity?) complete and determinate in itself that awaits to be realized through an occurring act.[9] It is an incomprehensible conception, which thinks of realization as of the extrinsic process of simple positing (a translation that changes *essentially* nothing) *in* or *as* reality an entity-essence that is diminished in itself and is paradoxically endowed with a nonexistential act of being. This is really a wrong way of thinking the difference between active and passive potentiality, in which the ability to receive a perfection becomes a determinate essence (potential content or set of contents). Conceiving of such an *entity as possible* implies a series of confusions regarding the entity's structure, among which are the impossibility of grasping potentiality as a co-principle of the entity or as a transcendental relation, and the confusion—explicit in Lévy—between reality and substance. The latter, for its part, leads to the positing of a structural difference between substance, as a synonym for "real," and event, which Lévy himself is at pains to mitigate. In fact, at the end of his book on the virtual, Lévy realizes that "the apparent dualism between substance and event may in fact hide a profound unity,"[10] and then acutely refers to Whitehead, for whom

> the final terms of philosophical analysis—that which truly exists—are events, are referred to as actual occasions. An actual

occasion is a kind of transitory monad, an elementary process of perception, generally unconscious, that receives certain data from previous actual occasions, interprets them, transmits them to other syntheses, and disappears.[11]

Lévy does not follow Whitehead any farther and proposes, by way of a general ontological principle, a substance-event connection that thinks the event as "a kind of molecular substance, miniaturized and fragmented," and symmetrically, substance as the "appearance of a set of events, a multitude of coordinated microexperiences aggregated into the image of a 'thing.'"[12] The reference to Whitehead's descriptive metaphysics is interesting in that some aspects of this theory seem to fit the description of an eminently interactive and structurally relational field, such as that of the virtual. For Whitehead the event, a node of multiple relations in becoming (bodies are for Whitehead sets of events and not material entities occupying a definite volume the same and equal for all observers), is neither physical nor mental, but rather a plexus of perceiver, perceived, and the relation between them. Events in turn structure complex nodes by self-intertwining with other events and taking on events as parts of themselves. So, they carry out the function of subject, but reversibly that of object when they are "taken on" as part of other events. Subject and object, active and passive, are therefore reversible procedural functions, that is, the subject is not *subjectum* or *substratum,* but, in the language of Whitehead, a superject, a provisional point-place that aggregates events and some spatio-temporal phases of the process. Historically, this ontology, which develops into a complex theory of "eternal objects," constructs metaphors that seek to structure a field coherent with a relativistic time-space.[13] For us, it is especially useful for interpreting not only the virtual body-environment in general, but also the difficult, albeit theoretically feasible, situation of encounter among those virtual bodies that are the avatars, which implies a subject-object reversibility in which the differentiation of bodies in the field—dimensions, volumes, forms, secondary and tertiary qualities included—takes place as the relative absence or presence of causal relations in continuous exchange. To use a metaphor derived from another tradition, the task is that of thinking of a constant deterritorialization of subjectivity and identity in general, without the latter disappearing entirely as horizon of experience. In other words, the issue is that of thinking of the points of exchange as intersections between identity and difference.

The notion of deterritorialization refers to Deleuze. It is straight out of *Difference and Repetition* that Pierre Lévy derives his problematic and banal notion of the possible, which he then sets up in opposition to the virtual. The virtual is a concept that shapes Deleuze's philosophy of the event. To try to delineate its significance would entail a confrontation with his philosophy as a whole, whereas we are simply interested in drawing from Deleuze's elaboration of the virtual some suggestions for an understanding of the virtual object as an interactive digital image. First of all, in Deleuze the virtual-possible contraposition is strategic with respect to the theme of time. The possible is conceived as "an image of the real,"[14] and is fabricated retrospectively, starting from the existing present. The real and the possible are therefore constituted by means of relations of resemblance in which difference is spun out of existence (in the present time) or presence. The virtual-actual pair is indicative of a different temporality, since virtuality is "the past's very being in itself,"[15] an *is* that does not really exist, is not present, yet is no mere negation or opposition. The virtual-actual pair expresses, in short, the gathering and therefore the contemporaneity of non-copresent spheres of being.[16] What is thus introduced is a difference within temporality in the form of a vacuum, a lacuna that cannot be made part of presence and delimits a spacing occurring within the event thereby avoiding its totalization: "In order to be actualized, the virtual . . . must *create* its own lines of actualization . . . while the real is in the image and likeness of the possible that it realizes, the actual on the other hand does *not* resemble the virtuality that it embodies. It is difference that is primary in the process of actualization."[17]

These are the Bergsonian themes of memory and duration translated into the dimension of the unusual. It is the exit from the modes of a temporality that maintains the opening within the totality of presence. This is what, at least at the most basic level, Deleuze calls the *virtual*. Virtuality allows that "not everything is given," allows "a positivity of time that is identical to a 'hesitation' of things and, in this way, to creation in the world. It is clear that there is a Whole of duration. But this whole is virtual."[18] So we have two elements that distinguish the virtual: a creative element, and a negative element, a kind of unmarking, or a "*not*," of presence that interrupts the linearity of relations of succession by introducing difference. The non-present virtual coexists with the actual, cutting into it as into a having-been, and therefore precisely because it coexists maintaining difference, it ensures that the actual does not resolve into presence. The interesting point here is that Deleuze brings to a remarkable level of profundity that which we have heretofore left unaddressed, namely, the relation between potentiality and novelty as an overlapping of past and future in the now or unity of experience. This is a relevant point for our comprehension of the interactive dynamic of the virtual image-body. Perhaps Deleuze's position attacks the potentiality-actuality dialectic, interpreting it as a possible-real dialectic (but the vocabulary is slippery, as sometimes Deleuze assimilates the virtual and the potential and does not oppose it to the real),[19] and thus fails to recognize the value of potentiality, excessively forcing the interpretation of the notion of the possible. Yet Deleuze has the merit of thinking of virtuality as nonorganic with respect to the sequence of past-present-future. The virtual-actual relationship is not one of succession and the virtual is not the originary, for if this were the case, then the actual would appear as a loss or degradation. Nor is the virtual thinkable as a not-yet, in which case the actual would represent improvement and perfection. What presents itself as an increase or loss, in short, as novelty, is read as a logic of differences or virtual distributions. The virtual-actual distinction must be thought of on a plane of univocal immanence[20] that "includes at the same time the virtual and its actualization. . . . The actual is the complement or product, the object of actualization, but this has as subject only the virtual."[21] In short, Deleuze thinks the virtual and actual as connected—*à la* Spinoza—in an expressive nexus, which has nothing to do with relations of analogy or forms of resemblance, and thanks to which "every object is double without it being the case that the two halves resemble one another, one being a virtual image and the other an actual image. They are unequal odd halves."[22]

The word *subject* used by Deleuze to indicate the virtual signifies simply time as a form of interiority free of subjectivity. It means memory, duration, difference with respect to any assimilation into chronological seriality. It means, in short, nonspatialized time as a sense of the virtual: "[T]he only subjectivity is time, non-chronological time grasped in its foundation, and it is we who are internal to time, not the other way around. . . . Subjectivity is never ours, it is time . . . the virtual."²³ It is [a kind of] time that is imprecise and unpredictable, anterior and posterior with respect to every sequence and movement, the disarticulation of order:

> It is the present that passes, that defines the actual. But the virtual appears, for its part, in a time smaller than that which measures the minimum movement in only one direction. This is because the virtual is "ephemeral". . . . The time smaller than the minimum thinkable in one continuous direction is also the longest time, longer than the maximum time thinkable in every direction. The present passes while the ephemeral preserves and is preserved. . . . Virtual entities communicate just above the actual by which they are separated.²⁴

All of this, I believe, can be taken as an effective description of an unusual field of experience constituted by the encounter between organic memory and computer memory, heterogeneous times of overlapping memories, between organic continuity and digital discreteness. It is a field in which the virtual is literally placed in a circle with the actual according to a deferment crystallized in perceptual experiences, percepts, or reciprocal holes in organic and digital bodies, subsisting as interactive events. It is clear that I understand the perpetual exchange of the virtual and the actual (in Deleuze's language called a "crystal") in a limited and distorted way as belonging to the virtual environment. In this way, general ontology is sucked into a region of entities, that is, into the region of the virtual event-objects, it becomes exemplary and nonpervasive, and it limits its power and truth. For Deleuze, "the relationship between the actual and the virtual is always a circle, but in two ways: sometimes the actual defers to the virtual as to other things in a vast circuit in which the virtual is actualized, and sometimes as the virtual proper in smaller circuits wherein the virtual is crystallized with the actual."²⁵ Our situation would be the second: the issue is that of singularities or singularizations through notable points that are to be determined on a case-by-case basis, that is, individuations constituted out of punctual relations between the actual and the virtual. In this context—the exploration of the notions of field and of singularity—Deleuze's concept of the virtual is useful because it illustrates the specific time-image interweaving.²⁶ Deleuze draws on film, but what he writes can be applied to the virtual image-body: when cinema combines actual image with memory-images, dream-images, and world-images, then the actual and the virtual enter into a circuit:

> Ever vaster circuits will be able to develop, corresponding to deeper and deeper layers of reality and higher and higher levels of memory and thought. But it is this most restricted circuit of the actual image and *its* virtual image which carries everything, and serves as internal limit . . . but this point of indiscernability is precisely constituted by the smallest circle, that is, the coalescence of the actual image and the virtual image.[27]

Such indiscernability is not confusion between the real and the imaginary, but rather an "objective illusion" in which real and imaginary, present and past, actual and virtual, acquire objectivity or existence. Now, Deleuze asks, "what are these consolidates of actual and virtual which define a crystalline structure (in a general, aesthetic, rather than scientific sense)?"[28] The easiest and most direct answer indicates the mirror image:

> [T]he mirror image is virtual in relation to the actual character that the mirror catches, but it is actual in the mirror which now leaves the character with only a virtuality and pushes him back out-of-field. The exchange is all the more active when the circuit refers to a polygon with a growing number of sides.[29]

The mirror allows for a reciprocal exchange, a virtual-actual circuit that results in reversibility between limpidity and opacity, clarity and obscurity. And the hermeneutic power of the crystal image, which Deleuze spins amidst great cinematic works so as to demonstrate their many faces in the expressive mirrors they constitute, is extraordinary. The crystallization of the time-image encounter is precisely what happens in the interactive and immersive experience of the virtual body, that is, the body that refers my acts to, that reflects them in, its own appearance, a simultaneously absorbent and reflective mirror that inaugurates the time in which memory becomes a phenomenon: "The present is the actual image, and *its* contemporaneous past is the virtual image, the image in a mirror."[30]

Interpreting in his own way the Bergson of *Matter and Memory*, Deleuze comes to establish the virtual image-time intertwining as the condition of possibility of temporality in general, venturing to think that "time consists of this split, and it is this, it is time, that we *see in the crystal*. The crystal-image was not time, but we see time in the crystal. We see in the crystal the perpetual foundation of time, non-chronological time, Cronos and not Chronos. This is the powerful, non-organic Life which grips the world."[31]

It seems to me that the circularity and inextricability of memory-time and dream-time, the coexistence of layers of the past and points of the present, the formation of an impersonal memory and the disruption of chronological succession, in a word: the virtuality of the time-image sometimes happens, takes body in certain works (on this Deleuze would agree), but finally amounts to experience as constitutive of the virtual body. The virtual body, even more than the movie screen (in its basic ontological structure and not on account of what is projected onto it) is, then, "the cerebral membrane where immediate and direct confrontations take place between the past and the future, the inside and the outside, at a distance impossible to determine, independent of any fixed point. . . . The image no longer has space and movement as its primary characteristics but topology and time."[32]

This multiple coexistence of times in the now speaks of an object that is event, and Deleuze does a good job of thinking the "event" side of the event-object. The event, for Deleuze, comes from chaos, that chaos against which philosophy, art, and science protect [us], and that is imagined as

> the infinite speed with which every form taking shape in it vanishes. It is a void that is not a nothingness but a *virtual*, containing all possible particles and drawing out all possible forms, which spring up only to disappear immediately, without consistency or reference, without consequence. Chaos is an infinite speed of birth and disappearance.[33]

From this "chaotic virtuality" emerges, through the movement of reflection, a "virtuality that has become consistent, that has become an entity formed on a plane of immanence that sections the chaos. This is what we call the Event,"[34] that is, a kind of pure reserve, latency, internality of the plane of immanence, which coincides with that non-instantaneous temporality that actualizes itself in the instant thereby disrupting, as has been noticed, its meaning of location-point in the order of succession.

The aspect of a gap[35] (lacuna, aperture, spacing, lack of determinacy) staged by the figure of chaos is interesting[36] and makes at last possible a return to the dimension of potentiality that belongs to the ontological structure of the virtual body as its co-principle. I would say that in the constitution of a reality that is not properly relational, the becoming of the entity, which is a *synolon* of potentiality and actuality, is an accentuation of the ambit of actuality, whereas in the case of the virtual body-event, insofar as this is an interaction, a phenomenon of relative determination, what emerges is rather a double potentiality. For this reason, the feature of ability, the ability to become, that is, the actual aspect of potentiality, is relevant only relatively, is relative to a different potentiality. When one observes the virtual body, one can see well that what is at work is a double potentiality of being real that exceeds the capacity in act. In short, there is a latency truly unknown, indeterminable by right (and not only in fact) through an analysis of the entity in act. This means that in the virtual entity potentiality can be grasped as an ontological void, a relative nonbeing within the entity, or, which amounts to the same, one notices that potentiality is a state *between* being and nonbeing. What can be seen less well is instead the *primacy* of actuality, that is, being as substance, permanence, identity, and so on.

7

The Virtual Actor-Spectator

As we have seen, the virtual has the peculiarity of being an intermediate entity between object and event, thing and image: "Virtual space is no longer an intelligible substrate. It is an object of modeling and constant interaction with other modeled objects. Virtual space, insofar as it is experienced, is therefore an image (the image of a model) and not a substantial reality."[1]

I do not think, as I hope to have shown, that the contraposition suggested by Quéau can be *simply* accepted.[2] It is important to remember, though, that virtual bodies are a *metaxu*,[3] intermediary entities that make up a hybrid, interactive world, visualizable as an image of syntheses, immersive, engaging the corporeality of the user, who mixes up with the image of the virtual body: "There occurs," Quéau correctly writes, "a deep hybridization between the body of the actor-spectator and the virtual space in which he or she is immersed."[4] It is time, then, to reflect on the idea of the actor-spectator.[5]

Now, it is obvious that the idea of "spectator," which is always internal to a theory, carries within itself the world, that is, a representational system, taste, social conventions, and philosophical convictions, in a word: culture. It carries not only all this, however, but also that which offers itself as a greater resistance to historical changes, such as sense perception and the emotional properties that cultural strategies seek to interpret. Above all, the theme of "the spectator" includes forms of the arts and their techniques, their ineluctable materiality, their evolution. The viewer of a painting is certainly not the same as the viewer of a photograph, as these are productions that lead, as do any artistic-technical type, to a different spatiotemporal plexus that affects the figure of the spectator. What does the spectator of a photograph expect from the ossification of passed time in the spatial plane of the now if not, as Barthes claims, the affective vision of an irrecoverable spectrum, and thus the pain of an impossible return? Conversely, paintings always seem to introduce a new game, less oriented to the confusion between reality of the past and truth, and more intended toward the imaginary of simulation and the modeling of the gaze in the closed spatial appropriation of temporal becoming. In the play of similarities and differences it is perhaps the analogy with cinema, because of its multimedia aspects, that allows us to approach the figure of the virtual spectator. In fact, new media are in general operations of remediation, or even "remediations of remediations" capable of displaying in a clear and amplified manner the tension between immediacy and hypermediacy: an immediacy, or transparency and removal of mediation that, in the maximum case constituted by virtual reality, is the result of a sophisticated process of hypermediation, which tends to conceal itself as such. Every new medium re-founds, re-mediates, the media that make it up in relation to the level or stratum of remediation that they produce. Hence, the cinema-virtual reality analogy highlighted by Bolter and Grusin exactly in relation to a specific spectatorial look: "One way to understand virtual reality, therefore, is as a remediation of the subjective style of film, an exercise in identification through occupying a visual point of view."[6] Of course, this is only a partial similarity. In a virtual environment, the spectator is the point of view, the eye of the camera, so to speak, and seems to have the power to decide what movements to perform with his or her eye. In reality, the eye, or better, the body, the mind-body complex is even in this case at least partially other-directed, but for now this is not the point. The point is to exploit the analogy in an effort to bring to light the differences by taking as our point of departure a field of research that has already been largely explored.

We are, above all, dealing with a simple, and I believe quite acceptable set of resemblances: like the cinematic image, the virtual image-body is the result of a complex mental process in which perception is never the simple recording of an external stimulus. But what we might call with Souriau the "spectatorial plane,"[7] that is, the place of realization of a specific view that is structured through interaction with certain data, is realized according to various modalities. To this end we can ask: How is the dialogue between work and spectator established in a virtual environment? Let us pause for a moment to reflect on cinema.[8] The shooting (shooting of reality: in any case, warrantee of objectivity, *greifen* and *begreifen, capere* and *concipere*)⁹ camera (warrantee of objectivity and mechanical laws) works so as to place the spectator's eye on a scale of distances arranged almost on a slope, such to produce the sliding of perspective within the scene. Seeing, knowing, and believing (that is, the eidetic, epistemic, and doxastic components) in this process of scaling are always intertwined and articulated. From objective shooting, that is, perspective of a no one, transparency in mediation, which is also the effect of a pure testimony, a neutral point of view on the world, we move to an unreal objective shooting that breaks up the verisimilitude of the relation between camera movement and eye movement, proposing frames or shots that are impossible for human beings, so that the medium becomes opaque and the spectator is summoned as an interpreter, called upon, paradoxically, to self-identify with the impossible perspective of the camera. Then, from here—along a path that progressively abandons the focus on diegesis in favor of developing a metadiscursive knowledge connected to modes of filming over and above content, until it arrives at the establishment of a partial, contingent, and in a sense dialogical communicative knowledge that constitutes the relinquishment of the epistemic view from nowhere—the view of the camera becomes, for example through the camera view of a character, an interpellation of the spectator. And finally, in subjective shooting, the viewer's gaze is sucked, so to speak, into the scene, and the spectator's vision, imagination, and knowledge come to coincide with those of a character. Having lost the universality of the third-person and the imperative of the second, the point of view returns to the *I*'s home, but it is a doubled, split *I* that knows both inside and outside of the text to the point that, as is well known, a film shot entirely in the subjective mode fails to provoke a definite illusion of immersion, and instead accentuates the presence of the camera. The paradoxicality of this situation signals a failure that belongs to the charm of cinema: that representation is to sustain itself at the limit of its cancellation. Cinema is here understood as the culmination of the history of perspective, of the objectifying point of view, of the distance and detachment that allow the contemplation of the world, truer to the extent that it is neutral, that is, to the degree that the material and cultural systems of mediation remain hidden in the fiction of cinematic operations. At its apex, this operation of removal comes to simulate the overcoming of distance by overcoming Alberti's window through the use of the subjective camera: that same eye that experienced the dizziness of becoming "all of the eye to all of the horizon" now penetrates into the world in front of it and inhabits, as it were, the painted scene. In many respects, then, cinema truly is the apex of the perspective view, but its value is also its limit: the qualitative and quantitative multiplication of points of view not only ends up not eliminating the point of view as such, but it also fails to elude distance. In any case, the effect of slipping into the picture is interrupted and the space of the screen is not inhabited. Movement and multiplicity, that is, the repudiation of the abstract fixity of the gaze, do not provoke an effective abandonment of distance, or a final immersion. Distance is essential precisely for the spectatorial status of the cinematic view, for the dynamics of desire that it puts to work. And the distance from the screen is that of a view forced into distance; it is a view that overlaps another view, the promise of ambiguous identifications, the feeling of intimacy with the stranger. The otherness projected onto the screen is, as it were, absorbed by the view of the spectator, who is compelled almost to intensify and accelerate profound mechanisms of self-projection and identification. The mechanical animation of images, the succession of phases provoking illusions of dynamism, blend seamlessly with the perceptual, almost magical and animistic animation of the image: it is a belief in the double, in metamorphosis and ubiquity, as recalled by Morin.[10]

We therefore know, to summarize, that perspectival vision seems natural to our cultural sensibilities, but it is substantially artificial, an activity of construction that imitates ocular vision: while it performs the mimetic operation, it institutes the modeling point of view. Insofar as the film camera descends from the *camera obscura,* cinema takes up this representational tradition, and filmic representation symbolically presupposes a viewing subject whose ocular vision is afforded a privileged place. [Cinema] certainly adds movement, and therefore narrative: that is, instability, performance, time, processes of identification (one could just think of the notion of "plane" and how it acts upon the apprehension of time and movement in the field). But none of these changes the essential distance from the screen and the essential perspectival dimension as constitutive of the art of reproducing three-dimensional space in two dimensions (we could think of the field's depth as an example of the strengthening of perceptual effects on the part of film equipment). All of this reinforces perspective as a form of illusion. Indeed, precisely the condemnation of distance and the illusion of its overcoming constitute in a remarkable manner cinema's grand charm, its duplicity often affirmed in delightful ways by the utilization of equipment, sometimes for the production of metalinguistic effects: one could just think of the use of plane-sequence, of the internal-external duality of the staging view, which constitutes a form of both realistic and antirealistic poetics. The mechanisms for the simulation of immersivity are thus quite interesting, in particular the operations and theories of the montage, along with the construction of narrative. Yet the "objective [lens]"and the "shooting camera [*macchina da presa*]" remain, and the immersion is always postponed. Now, this postponement is preserved, it seems to me, in Internet art and perhaps, for partially different reasons, in a large variety of digital art (I do not intend to discuss the term *art*, I simply take it here as if it were known). The computer, the processor is at this level a meta-medium, a mediation of a mediation, as Bolter and Grusin wish to maintain, and it rearticulates and deepens, as we said, the tension between immediacy and hypermediacy. There are, however, profound differences between cinematic spectator and consumer of the virtual environment. The latter is not seated on a chair (and, in the case of cinema, immobilized in the dark), resting before a screen on which a parade of two-dimensional animated images is displayed, whose animation provides an illusion of continuity and movement offering for consumption a simulacrum of the perception of reality. Above all, such a consumer's view is not split in two by the other eye of the film camera. The virtual consumer feels and acts in a sensibly complex environment that is not simulacral, not image of, because virtual bodies literally refer to their nonbeing, to algorithms, to scripts: in brief, they are bodies whose nonbiological genesis is reproducible, bodies generated by intelligences and other bodies; they are not mimetic reproductions that can unfold infinitely. On the one hand, if the virtual environment does not imply the co-presence of multiple human actors, nevertheless the consumer, like the cinema spectator, can still self-identify with his or her own view as with the focus of representation, as the privileged subject of vision: the consumer sees the environment from his or her point of view, and the representation (but is it even still "representation"?) of the environment is organized through the nonprecise, but partially dynamic and unique viewpoint of his or her own body. In the virtual environment this happens only partially, as spatiality and interaction work as function of rupture of the primary identification between the self and the self's own perspective. The virtual environment is in fact first and foremost a spatial environment that is never simply geometric and perspectival space, but is, rather, formed as movement and is not other from the oculomotorious and kinesthetic space. It is a space that lives from both the movement of the user's body and the interactivity between user and virtual body. In this space, "things" do not fill the space, but are rather qualitative concretions that appear, phenomena that exist by means of interaction. Clearly, the topological properties of such a space should be investigated carefully, but they are not natural and univocal insofar as they are (at least partially yet consistently) products of the interaction, and the latter is not only, perhaps not even primarily, a physical fact, but concerns instead expectations and desires, actions and volitions.

Now, we can ask ourselves precisely what sort of subject-spectator is brought about by the virtual device. As mentioned above, contrary to what happens for the cinematic spectator, what occurs here is the encouragement and nonsuspension of motility, the superinvestment of kinesthetic functions, the feeling of inclusion before the scene, the simultaneous feeling of differentiation and inclusion with the characters of the scene of which the user is part, because the scene as such would not exist without the user's action. The voyeuristic impulse is replaced with a drive toward insertion, toward intervention without limits, toward omnipotence frustrated only by the limits of the program. What is the metapsychological regime of virtual immersion? What are the processes of the I's identification, imaginary constitution, and differentiation? Saturation seems to be characteristic of the virtual environment: the effect of filling, of presence, as has been said above, and not of absence and distance. The spectator does not arise as a subject in a state of lack, which is virtual only in terms of potentiality. There is no suspension of reality, but rather the presence of another reality, not as a shelter from reality, but as its increase. What is cut off is precisely the aspect of regression and suspension of reality, and therefore, ultimately, the possibility—always plural—of self-identifying with what is represented, in particular, with the characters represented: the immersion makes the sense of alterity be too strong to enable projection as identification. The virtual spectator cannot self-identify with the subject of his or her vision-action. Now, this cutting off of primary identification entails the cutting off, at a certain level, of the processes of secondary identification, which have to do mainly with the different temporality belonging to the virtual. Identity is always constituted out of a multitude of identifications, it is the provisional place of a partial, contingent, often conflictual synthesis, of more or less heterogeneous images of one's self. Undoubtedly, the novel, theater, and cinema, through the staging of the other as a figure of the same, have played a significant role in secondary identification, turning, so to speak, the I into a building site, constructing the ideal of the I through its identification with various, sometimes diverse, and partly contradictory models. Such genres have been able to perform these operations because, fundamentally, they have staged stories, have suspended their spectators-readers to the stories themselves, have projected their desire of entering the stories into a structured plot of embracing and pervasive relations, an entanglement of compelling presences and absences, in front of which the reader-viewer is almost forced to renounce, at least momentarily, awareness of his or her own self and to find again his or her own identity—augmented, deconstructed, in short, different—at the end of the reading or viewing. As we know, these processes of identification depend on structural operations connected to the art of storytelling, operations which in themselves prescind from psychology yet produce psychological effects. The classic novel, in its unfolding through successive situations, provokes a relatively stable identification. So too does narrative cinema, because the variability of viewpoints is inscribed in its code so that the scene is constructed upon a multiplicity of viewpoints such as to suggest to the spectator's view privileged paths that seem, even when this is false, to unfold continuously for the spectatorial view in a homogeneous space. In both [narrative cinema and classic novel], each and every point of view is inscribed in a hierarchy, in a completely predictable and finite relational network.

What story is possible for virtual art, though? The equipment does not allow for the complete predictability of patterns of narration because the interaction, while limited by the logical space of the programming, disrupts the temporal linearity of the story, introducing into it the dense and often undefined package of the user's always partially unpredictable action.[11] Using a metaphor, one could say that it introduces into the system a certain degree of freedom that is sufficient to upset, literally, the order of the narration. It is no longer a closed text with beginning and end, but rather a text whose ending is interruption, is contingent. One could even say that without order and internal consistency, even if arranged along multiple lines (as in the case of a hypertext that is offline or is in any case complete even if the story remains open to multiple possible endings), there is no narrative, and that the virtual device is therefore not narrative. This implies a disarticulation of the relation between utterance and what is uttered, as the abstract and invisible place in which the strategies, the grammar, and rhythm of the work are carried out is not a narrative instance that remains concealed from the eyes of the spectator. This can still result in a story, in a set of meanings, but it is a story that is not narration. It is a complex of material elements (*materia subtilis* or virtual body) that is not endowed with a predetermined sense, yet constitutes a nonautonomous existence of its own. It is a world under construction and not a pseudo-world or fictional universe, a virtual reality and not a simulacrum of reality. It is a story, in short, for which one is not given a script. Thus, what essentially changes in virtual reality is the sense of the fundamental cinematic operation, namely, the sense of the montage. In fact, aside from the underlying metaphysical considerations, for which the operations of montage can either be condemned because they fail to meet the extraordinary and fascinating ambiguity of the real (Bazin)[12] or exalted because they give meaning to a reality that is otherwise amorphous or even nonexistent in itself (Sergei Eisenstein),[13] in cinema montage manipulates levels—ordering their succession and fixing their duration—to the (syntactical, semantic, temporal) goal of narrative construction. It is thanks to montage that the cinematic spectator knows without seeing and learns, through associative modes, features that are foreign to images individually considered. Now, even if montage may not have a connection to narrative, nevertheless it is still related, in cinema, to the unfolding of the image in the time-space of the film's unidirectional running. In other words, the montage limits the unpredictability of the real and forces it to take up a sense that unfolds linearly in time-space. In virtual reality, by contrast, what we call operations of "montage" must predict, although they cannot do so completely, the modification of the environment caused by the user's interaction. The rules governing montage in virtual reality thus have the task, truly at the very limits of possibility, of simulating the ambiguity of the real. The ontological model here presupposed is then mixed, [lies] between the ambiguity immanent to the real and the reflection, through programming, of operations of cutting and editing, that is, of the institution of meaning, of reflection upon the real. Computer "montage" is then indeed a principle that produces meaning, though a fragile meaning.

What is it that posits virtual reality as aesthetic? Is it perhaps the possibility of performing a transformation of reality into an imaginary object subjected to a poetic that alters, in a Kantian manner, time, space, and causality? Or, is it the possibility of performing a simulation of reality that contains its own negation: a tendentially perfect reproduction that denounces its own failure, and therefore its own ambiguity, uncertainty, and, what is more, the unpredictable internal dynamism belonging to its own peculiar materiality? Or even, is it a return to physical and therefore aesthetic reality, powerful as to the effects of its qualitative content? In any case, unlike in classic cinema and in this respect similar to some performances and forms of contemporary theater, in virtual art the work is not perceived as a zero grade of enunciation or as a "natural" mode; rather, it is precisely the maximum degree of simulation that testifies to the maximum level of artificiality. Virtual art appears as an art form (which includes but is not limited to the audiovisual) whose productive equipment implies the task not of shaping the spectator's view, of modeling the currents of his or her desire, but rather of corresponding to this view and these currents by integrating itself with them, allowing itself to be changed and modified to the extent that it changes and modifies them. It is the idea of an ecstasis with return, or better, of the simultaneous coincidence of the two: an exit from oneself, and then an affective and intellectual adhesion, in a way that can change the meaning of the event. As mentioned above, we are therefore close to some forms of contemporary theater and certain art forms that incorporate events, but within a spatiotemporal environment closer to that of dreams, so as to dispel the controversy between those who believe in the image and those who believe in reality. "Presence," the very sensation of presence, the immersion into a virtual environment, is indeed a strange phenomenon. Even in "real" environments, the presence of bodies is partially subjected to the psychological and cultural complexities of the consumer. The environment-bodies [*corpi-ambiente*] are instead external in a rather strong sense, such that they cannot be amended simply by virtue of the being-there of these complexities: they have a resistance of their own, so to speak, an irreducible alterity. This alterity of the environment-body assumes more fluid characteristics in the virtual environment because virtual bodies are ontologically both internal and external and refer, in the final analysis and through sophisticated and accidental mediations, to a dialogue between user and programmer. We have here both heterodirectionality and autodirectionality: an awareness of the artificiality of the time-space and the bodies therein, as well as a spontaneous involvement with them whose degree of intensity depends upon the technical complexity of the artifice. One can understand the experience of the virtual, in this sense, as an extension of the experience of the film viewer. Whereas cinema is living image, to put it in Morin's terms, and, as representation of living representation, it invites us to reflect upon the imaginary character of reality and upon the reality of the imaginary, in the case of the virtual the elaboration of the body of the imaginary enables us to reflect upon *representation* as *reality* in itself. Maybe it is true that the fact of representing something suggests an at least implicit will to affirm, to speak, to utter, to produce in some fashion a discourse; in the case of virtual art, though, can one speak of "representation"? It is clear that at this point at least two paths open up: one direction, which follows Gibson's theory of visual perception, could be named ecological, and prompts us to interpret the qualities of immersion and interaction avoiding the belief that the consumer is a system of information processing in representational terms; another avenue would lead us to a speculative rereading of the forms of figurative art as non-narrative and nonmimetic, following here well-known theories from Lyotard to Deleuze. But what does it mean, in the case of virtual art, to speak of nonrepresentation and non-narrativity? It simply means, as we have already seen, that virtual bodies do not represent anything beyond themselves, are (digital) images but not images of anything other, and are thus strictly speaking not representations, but image-entities [*enti-immagini*]. It also means that the narratives that unfold in the virtual environment are problems-in-progress, and not plots that develop within the time-space of causal relations out of an intensity or a plexus that pre-encompasses them (according to the model of beginning state/transformations/final state). In other words, from the ontological point of view, virtual bodies are events, or better, actions-events [*eventi-azioni*], where the divide, the space marked by the hyphen that both joins and divides, cannot be identified with precision. The spectator too becomes then an actor and reciprocally, insofar as actor, he or she is also spectator: spectator-actor, active-passive, potential-actual, that is, in a word, virtual.

8

For an Aesthetics of the Hypertext

It seems very easy to define the hypertext.¹ For Landow, for example:

> *Hypertext*, a term coined by Theodor H. Nelson in the 1960s, refers also to a form of electronic text, a radically new information technology, and a mode of publication. "By hypertext," Nelson explains, "I mean non-sequential writing—text that branches and allows choices to the reader, best read at an interactive screen. As popularly conceived, this is a series of text chunks connected by links which offer the reader different pathways." *Hypertext,* as the term is used in this work, denotes text composed of blocks of text—what Barthes terms a lexia—and the electronic links that join them. . . . Electronic links connect lexias "external" to a work—say, commentary on it by another author or parallel or contrasting texts—as well as within it and thereby create text that is experienced as nonlinear, or, more properly, as multilinear or multisequential.²

Naturally, the chunks connected by links can include not only verbal data, and so hypertext is also hypermedia. Now, as we know, from this definition Landow traces out some interesting consequences at the level of theory, such as to involve notable and rather diverse contributions from the likes of Foucault, Bakhtin, Barthes, and Derrida. There remains, however, the problem, which implies other issues, of the opposition between *nonlinearity* and *multilinearity*. The *multilinear* is a quantitative strengthening of the *linear* in the same way that the *multisequential* is a strengthening of the *sequential*. So if hypertext really is multilinear text, then far from representing and experimenting models of nonlinear inscription, writing, or thought, it actually confirms and reinforces the usual models of linear production. There is an interesting note in Landow's book regarding nonlinear thinking:

> Dorothy Lee finds an exception to linearity in the language of Trobriand Islanders, which reveals that they "do not describe their activity lineally, they do no dynamic relating of acts; they do not use even so innocuous a connective as *and*." According to Lee, they do not use causal connections in their descriptions of reality, and "where valued activity is concerned, the Trobrianders do not act on an assumption of lineality at any level."
> . . . Appropriately, therefore, when an inhabitant of the Trobriand Islands "relates happenings, there is no developmental arrangement, no building up of emotional tone. His stories have no plot, no lineal development, no climax."[3]

I am convinced that thinking is neither linear nor sequential but is, so to speak, a diffuse center, whereas verbal language, as discrete, can only be linear and sequential (except for certain exceptional cases, which are exceptionally interesting to study).[4] But any hypertext, and especially narrative hypertext, acts in a manner precisely opposite: from any (programmed) point (the inevitable "start," in the sense that even if there are many possible beginnings that are always already programmed in their possibility, nevertheless the start will always be one of many) there start causal connections that proliferate patterns, which can develop toward a climax or, obviously, choose a different strategy for the device, but always in a "linear" way. From this point of view, narratology can rest easily: the old categories (fable, narration, plot, and so on) also work for hypertext.[5] The relevance of these categories, however, can become more complicated, because hypertext (narrative hypertext in particular) realizes certain possibilities, that is, certain possible worlds permitted by the text, and is ultimately an exhibition of the multiplication of possibilities: it is an exhibition in the proper sense because it brings out the trace of its own rules of constitution. This, on the one hand, provokes an inevitable and essentially importunate interruption of transparency, interrupting a fiction that one would always want to be as mimetic as possible, an exposure of the technical operations of the scene (not of the author, as hypertext is always a product of teamwork, carried out at varying levels of competence), and on the other, it conversely provokes in the consumer a sense of freedom, which is simply the positive aspect of the well-known effect of disorientation in the navigation of hypertext. We are now faced with two questions that converge into one: the question of what belongs to the hypertext with respect to its enjoyment, or, if one prefers, of what potentialities of formatting on the part of the navigator belong to the hypertext.

We can put the first question as follows: Do excesses in quantity (the quantity of possible paths, of the multilinearity whose programming is made possible by the hypertext's electronic substance) lead to changes in quality? I think we can say that the construction of a hypertext as opposed to the construction of a text implies an excess of creativity, an excess that consists, in my view, not so much in the solicitation of many sensory channels (the hypermedial aspect of hypertext), or in the growth of interactivity, but simply in the building of links between chunks. Hypertext is text in electronic format that contains clickable links, and it is perhaps the more creative the less these links carry out a merely utilitarian function. That is to say, the more these clickable links, these buttons, build a system of relations, a system of connections, that tend to augment the complexity of the system's meaning, the more the hypertext will be afforded an aesthetic quality. Hypertext can be thus thought in accordance with an organic metaphor, as a system of relations in which it is precisely relations that constitute the accrued value because the functionality of the system's components depend on them and therefore [it unfolds] in accordance with a law of immanent formativity, that is, as a self-regulating system formatted by the user as a condition of possibility for interactivity. From this point of view, hypertext is a decidedly classical aesthetic machine. We could define it as an "*oratio sensitiva perfecta*" [perfect sensuous speech], which, as we know, is the definition of the poem as it is offered by Baumgarten in his *Meditationes de nonnullis ad poema pertinentibus*.[6] But, more precisely, hypertext would be a perfect cognitive-sensory oration, which is the one whose parts tend toward knowledge of cognitive-sensory representations, and which is made the more perfect the greater number of parts act so as to give rise to such cognitive-sensory representations. This is precisely what hypertext produces in its dimension of hypermediality. Now, perfection is consensus in variety, where the term *consensus* must be taken in its relational and purposive sense: consensus of the many to one insofar as the many constitute the sufficient reason of such one. It is the idea, then, of architectonic functionality: the one to which the many parts consent is, as we have seen, the production of cognitive-sensory representations, and because the various parts themselves are cognitive-sensory representations, their meaning consists in stimulating others. In distended but controlled progress, the hypertext generates ever-new representations. It produces, or should produce, the pleasure of or interest in navigation (sweet surfing . . .). At this point, the task is not so much arguing the case for a poetics of hypertext, with its *facultas fingendi* and peculiar ghosts, as it is grasping its theoretical sense. Increasingly so, and increasingly to the extent that it is born as such, that is, insofar as it is original and creative (as is the case for narrative hypertext), hypertext emerges from a constructive process, not by means of the breaking down, deconstruction, or fragmentation of a text, but from the construction of screens through the connecting of objects, which are perhaps lexias only in a few cases (sometimes they are not even sensory representations). What matters then is the quality of the objects, chunks, or elements on which the power of technology is concentrated, and especially the structure or coherence, as relative to the links and their theme, on which the strength of the theory is focused. I am not interested here in the problems of internal syntax (that is, whether it is internal or external), but in the concept of "link," that is, in the status of the relation. Now, the link is a sensed connection: it is the relation for which the mutual agreeing of the elements is implemented. No link in the hypertext can be sterile, barren: the hypertext is an environment in which the elements are linked together in a succession that appears as a suture, in a basically smooth manner that is however interrupted by the sensibility of portions of the screen. The hypertext can take shape, however, that is, it can complete itself as a structure, if in it there exists a theme, *propositum,* or *argumentum,* that may constitute a sufficient reason for the elements or sensible representations that compose it (it is at this level, however difficult it may be to identify it clearly, that one poses the question as to what "literary" genre the hypertext belongs).

It is clear at this point that the hypertext is an efficacious metaphor for the world. If we map the space of this world we have a physical space, a logical space, and various representative spaces, expressed or phenomenalized (what appears on the screen), implicit or virtual (possible linkages of or from the screen, and therefore the inter- and intra-textual net), and finally a phatic space that connects and maintains the user's connection and so is primarily symbolic precisely in its appearance, in the form it takes on in order to format the moves of the interaction.[7] What interests me is not the rhetorical aspect, but the logical space (which explains the metaphor of the world), which corresponds to the level of the invisible, of that which is a condition for the possibility of representation; that is, it corresponds to the conceptual architecture whereby the elements are organized, to that structure that constitutes the place of inscription of the hypertext's component parts, and which, understood in its purposive sense, I have called "theme." Now, the logical space is the place of the actual writing of the hypertext from the point of view of meaning. It is a metatextual place in which the texts of hypertext are mediated. The logic of this space is, as previously mentioned, multilinear, but multiplicity is here a qualitative value insofar as it produces in the consumer, that is, the reader-viewer-listener, an effect of freedom. Far from being anarchic, hypertextual space is equipped with such sophisticated organization that it produces an effect of freedom, and this constitutes a certain philosophical image of the world, the complexity of which makes us believe that we are operating free choices.

I do not ask myself questions here regarding the logic of the logical space, which is a spatial logic of reticular association, a topology that works mostly according to the principle of proximity, but, in any case, in which "the attribution of references and the understanding of meaning are continually suspended until the entire pattern of internal references cannot be grasped as a unity."[8] I am instead interested in stressing that the hypertext constitutes a certain type of theological image of the world. The hypertext's plural Author is a *Deus absconditus,* a transcendent God more than a programming watchmaker, who predetermines the possible paths and choices while building through their quantity an effect, as mentioned above, of freedom. It is important to notice that in traditional hypertext (let us say, *offline*) the virtual power of the connections is high, but not infinite: if it were infinite, then the logical structure as well as the sense of freedom associated with this connection would change. Thus, we have a reinforcement of the role of the author, but of an author in absence.

Up until now I have presented the concept of the creator-poet from Leibniz's and Wolff's aesthetological tradition, which, when brought to its hyperbole, leads to Baumgarten's *mundus poetarum* [world of poets]. In terms of judgment, the issue is to evaluate the concept of the project, the teleology of the hypertextual structure, that is, the theme.

But if we depart from the old offline hypertext and expand instead to consider the hypertext on the Web, what happens? What if, in addition to the hypertext, we introduce the Text Transfer Protocol in the World Wide Web environment?

As we have seen, offline hypertext altogether speaks a kind of monotheism. Even if the author is collective or multiple, this means only that it is not configured out of a strong identity or subjectivity, which in some respects is an interesting invention of modernity. After all, a single God can even host an inherent plurality.

The Web, conversely, is polytheist, is a pagan space wherein there are many gods, and so is a space upon which one is not afforded a single bird's-eye view: no hyper-author can have a totalizing view of the Internet. This does not mean an absolute gaining of freedom, but certainly a heightened sense of freedom on the part of the user, even if he or she always moves over a partial number of locations. Therefore, Web-based hypertext entails more theoretical problems: first of all, the fraying of limit. I have been able to consider hypertext in terms of a relatively classical work of art because it was complete: completeness is a condition of possibility for a scale of perfection, and thus for a traditional modality of aesthetic valuation. Indeed, the work of art is that which is complete, unique, original, closed in and for its novelty also and precisely in the multiplicity of rules. Yet the work of art as work, *this* finite work, is always infinite as the bearer of an essentially ambiguous truth, which at the same time remains itself and is always other than in itself in the plurality of interpretations. What interpretation is possible, however, of a hypertext frayed across the Web, whose connections are quantitatively finite but in effect (by means of its effects) infinite from the user's point of view, a hypertext whose limits or boundaries are continuously thinning and melting in the play of surfing within openings that cannot be dominated by any logic other than the plural logic of usefulness and desire? Perhaps, though I do not know the answer to this question, online hypertext is not essentially different from the offline variety, but—and this is what matters for our purposes—it better shows some conceptual things. I will mention only two. The first point still regards temporality, obviously as an effect of interactivity, or better, its perception through space: we know that the enjoyment of elements on a screen of hypertext occurs on a basic level in parallel, at a glance, and the elements are codified instantaneously by the brain. In short, we are faced with a complex, iconic text, the perception of which is analyzable, for example, at the level of planar topology. This first instantaneous glance is, however, joined almost immediately by a sequential fruition. In online hypertext, this double process is stretched in an indefinite perceptual-temporal environment. This, it seems to me, shakes the apparently unbroken evidence of the present as a form of time. In the kind of immersive experience that constitutes Web navigation, time is really felt as a "time not gathered," as a time always tormented by disjunction, by a postponement that is itself the "place" of otherness and that is introduced in the same instant as perception. The second point concerns the notion of world. The Internet is a continuously expanding set that modifies and at the same time is modified by its users. Its points of view, which are always within the net because an external point of view, be it universal or true, can never exist, are both non-finite and definite, since they are nothing other than relations in constant mutation. In this system essentially devoid of truth, the world seems to be thought of as a relational structure within time-space, and to be potentially infinitely multiplied across the net, both expressive and representative of interactions and connections. This world is total in character: in its dynamism, every possibility that can be actualized is actualized, but it is not endowed with any teleology, inasmuch as a dominant, external view is not possible. It is thus the case of a further and alternative metaphor for world.

A further step with regard to the topic of online hypertext—about which we can say something for diversion's sake and only on the level of a thought-experiment given the current insufficiency of technology—concerns the concept of cyberspace and especially the concept of the virtual, or better, of "virtual reality," a notion of remarkable conceptual density that is not easily studied (one could simply think of the problem of determining the notion of faithfulness with respect to virtual reality). These concepts are of particular interest for aesthetics because they involve corporeality in complex with intelligence. In my view, the modalities of experience in which mind and body are inextricable belong to the domain of study proper to aesthetics, and I believe that one can think well-known concepts such as collective intelligence and connective intelligence only in relation to the virtual modes of corporeality. Hypertext in cyberspace should then be considered as a sensible-cognitive environment beyond what is now technically possible. I would for now define this environment as haptic space.[9] Haptic space is not optical, is not an organization that founds appearance by outlining and deframing it according, for example, to perspectival laws. Nor is it a tactile space, which in a certain way dulls visual intelligence by means of a focus on sensibility, subordinating, so to speak, the eye to the hand. It is, rather, a place of integration, in which the eye touches the environment and the hand sees things in a continuous reversibility. We are thus faced with a further metaphor for world, in which the maximum of artificiality enables us to approach nature: the world no longer stands before us through representation; rather, it is born, so to speak, in the things of the world. Obviously, on this point I am paraphrasing Merleau-Ponty's *Eye and Mind*. Essence and existence, imaginary and real, visible and invisible: the virtual hypertext confounds all of our categories deploying its dreamlike universe of carnal essences, effective resemblances, and mute significations.[10]

Notes

INTRODUCTION

1. See Amihud Gilead, "How Many Pure Possibilities are There?" *Metaphysica. International Journal for Ontology and Metaphysics* 5, no. 2 (2004): 89–90; precisely, the "submarine" described by Jules Verne in *Twenty Thousand Leagues Under the Sea* is to be considered a "possible." Gilead is thus in debate with Nicholas Rescher, "Nonexistents Then and Now," *Review of Metaphysics* 57 (2003): 359–81.
2. Maurice Merleau-Ponty, "Eye and Mind," in *The Merleau-Ponty Reader*, ed. Leonard Lawlor and Ted Toadvine (Evanston: Northwestern University Press, 2007), 375.

CHAPTER 1. AESTHETICS OF THE VIRTUAL BODY

1. For a deep presentation of this notion, see the forum on digital images in the online magazine *Kainós* (www. Kainós.it) coordinated by Vincenzo Cuomo. Many interesting reflections on the topic of multimedia art, and numerous monographs from the magazine *Ligeia* 45–48 (July-Dec. 2003), edited by M. Costa and G. Lista, can be found here.
2. On this point, see Mario Costa, *Il sublime tecnologico* (Rome: Castelvecchi, 1998), 71.
3. If one means by "simulacra" a mimetic relationship in which the object is portrayed as infinite, then the structure of the simulacrum is built on the structure of mimesis: a deferment lacking in

originality, but in which the origin or model remains as absent, without negating the idea of origin or the relation to the origin as a model.
4. Unless the icon is thought of as a kind of threshold, relational place, transit, or exchange.
5. On the structure of synthetic images, see Michael Porchet, *La production industrielle de l'image. Critique de l'image de synthese* (Paris-Budapest-Turin: L'Harmattan, 2002), esp. 95–115.
6. Pietro Montani has opportunely insisted on this hard type of interactivity in a contribution to the meeting on "Estetica & Design" (Palermo, September 27, 2003), promoted by the SIE Laboratory of Industrial Design, directed by Luigi Russo. Obviously, interaction with the matrix is conceivable according to different modalities in relation to the type of virtual bodies with which one is interacting.
7. See Ralph Schroeder, ed., *The Social Life of Avatars. Presence and Interaction in Shared Visual Environments* (London: Springer Verlag, 2002); T. K. Sapin, I. S. Pandzic, N. Magnenat-Thalmann, and D. Thalmann, *Avatars in Networked Virtual Environments* (Chichester-New York: John Wiley and Sons, 1999).
8. An evolved example that demonstrates the potential in using avatars is *Gulliver's Box*, an interactive game system designed by research groups from the University of Singapore and the University of Osaka in collaboration with Futurelab of Electronic Arts, presented to the 2003 Electronic Arts Festival in Linz. The game is a kind of Mixed Reality application that generates a recreational environment. It allows entrance into the narrative world of *Gulliver's Travels,* where one chooses a persona and moves it within the scene through a glass cube placed on a table: the actions of the persona (Lilliputian, Brobdingagian), are reproduced on the display and set in a world of 3-D fantasy visible through an appropriate viewer; the characters can interact with one another in various movements and modify the point of view of the scene. What is thus realized is a perceptual experience in which the interaction between user, avatar, virtual environment, and physical environment produces engrossing combinations.
9. They should keep in mind Merleau-Ponty's *Phenomenology of Perception* (New York: Routledge, 1989).
10. An immaterial sculpture prototype whose development was

initiated by the *Polo didattico e di ricerca di Crema* at the University of Milan (coordinated by Gianni Degli Antoni) is described by Diana Danelli, *Per una scultura digitale a bassa densità*, in *Nel foco che li affina. Quattro studi per Francesco Piselli* (Milan: Prometheus, 2000), 23–44.

11. Perhaps immaterial sculpture can be considered a momentary point of arrival and a current place for researching a recognizable tendency in the electronic arts, which is made apparent in the catalogues of the Electronic Arts Festival in Linz. One is reminded, for example, of Karl Simms's at this time rather old (1993) *Genetische Bilder*, and of *Simulationsraum-Mosaik mobiler Datenklange-SD-MK* of the group KR+cF, or of Jeffrey Shaw's famous *Golden Calf*. It is likely that the more significant developments in digital art are to be found in the intersection between art on the Internet and art offline. For a general panorama of digital art, see: Lorenzo Taiuti, *Corpi sognanti. L'arte nell'epoca delle tecnologie digitali* (Milan: Feltrinelli, 2001); Christiane Paul, *Digital Art* (London: Thames and Hudson, 2003); Florence de Méredieu, *Arts et nouvelles technologies. Art vidéo Art numérique* (Paris: Larousse, 2003). In terms of virtual art in particular, see: Oliver Grau, *Virtual Art: From Illusion to Immersion* (Cambridge: MIT Press, 2003). For an accurate analysis of such works and poetics, see: Edmond Couchot and Norbert Hillaire, *L'art numérique* (Paris: Flammarion, 2003), and also Anne-Marie Duguet, *Dejouer l'image. Créations électroniques et numériques* (Nîmes: Jacqueline Chambon, 2002), especially for an interpretation of Jeffrey Shaw's works.

12. I am here using the terminology used by J. Steuer, "Definire la realtà virtuale: le dimensioni che determinano la telepresenza," in *La comunicazione virtuale. Dal computer alle reti telematiche: nuove forme di interazione sociale*, ed. C. Galimberti and Giuseppe Riva (Milan: Guerini and Associates, 1997), 55–78.

13. I am not dealing here with the theme of multimediality, which merits a deeper analysis. For a precise definition (in terms of "multiple digitized representation") and an articulation of its formative potentialities, see Pier Cesare Rivoltella, "La multimedialità," in *Tecniche e significati. Linee per una nuova didattica formativa*, ed. C. Seurati (Milan: Vita e Pensiero, 2000), 219–58.

14. Ibid., 65.
15. Ibid., 70.

16. Ibid., 71.
17. *Virtual Art*, op. cit., 15. On the different types of immersion, see Michael Heim, *Virtual Realism* (New York: Oxford University Press, 1998), 17–19 (on the immersion of the Cave system, see 20–22). For a deepening of the notion of immersion understood as the "sensation of being in an environment," see: William R. Sherman and Alan B. Craig, *Understanding Virtual Reality. Interface, Application, and Design* (Amsterdam: Morgan Kaufmann Publishers, 2003), 381–98.
18. On the aspects connected to sense perception in virtual environments, see Sherman-Craig, *Understanding Virtual Reality*, 205–80; Ken Hillis, *Digital Sensation. Space, Identity, and Embodiment in Virtual Reality* (Minneapolis: University of Minnesota Press, 1999), 90–131. With respect to the construction of a "sense of being in presence," there is an interesting article by John R. Wilson, "Towards Real Applications of Virtual Environments: Ergonomics Research and Development," in *Virtual Reality. Select Issues and Applications*, ed. H. M. Khalid (London: ASEAN Academic Press, 2000), 9–27 (see esp. 13–19). We shall analyze this problem in the following chapter.
19. The term *fedeltà* means faithfulness but also truthfulness, loyalty, accuracy. Its rendering with "faithfulness" and its cognates seems preferable in this context because of the connection with faith/belief [editor's note].
20. David Deutsch makes this point well in *The Fabric of Reality: The Science of Parallel Universes—and its Implications* (New York: Penguin, 1997), 113.
21. "Specifying a virtual reality environment does not mean specifying what the user will experience, but rather specifying how the environment would respond to each of the user's possible actions." Ibid.
22. Giovanni Ventimiglia brings to light another interesting aspect of the nonsimulative nature of the virtual: "the tendentious exemption of the negative," see Giovanni Ventimiglia, "Ontologia ed etica del virtuale," *Teoria* xxiv, no. 1 (2004): 119–47.
23. It is in this direction that "simulation" is understood by Philippe Quéau, *Eloge de la simulation* (Seyssel: Champ Vallon-INA, 1986), for example 238–39.
24. Philippe Quéau, "Les vois virtuelles du savoir," in *Costruzione e*

appropriazione del sapere nei nuovi scenari tecnologici, ed. A. Piromalla Gambardella (Naples: CUEN, 1998), 158.
25. To this end Jean-Louis Weissberg has written aptly of a "real/virtual compact"; see "Il compatto reale/virtuale," in *La scena immateriale. Linguaggi elettronici e mondi virtuali,* ed. A. Ferraro and G. Montagano (Milan: Cortina, 1998), 130.
26. Pierre Lévy, *Becoming the Virtual* (New York: Basic Books, 1998), 172.
27. See ibid. 24. Lévy references Deleuze's *Difference and Repetition.* Michael Heim prefers to invoke Duns Scotus: Scotus "maintained that the concept of a thing contains empirical attributes not in a formal way, but virtually.... Scotus used the term 'virtual' in order to bridge the gap between formally unified reality (as defined by our conceptual expectations) and our messily diverse experiences"; see Michael Heim, *The Metaphysics of Virtual Reality* (Oxford: Oxford University Press, 1993), 132. Eric Alliez also makes reference, in a suggestive way, to Duns Scotus, but in particular to the notion of *potentia absoluta,* absolute potential, in order to establish "the possibility of a perception (or of an intellection) contemporary to the 'projection' of an object prefigured with the former only in the programmed reduction of the entity to its concept"; see Eric Alliez, "Pour une phénoménology réelle des images virtuelles," *Chimeres* (Hiver 1996): 132.
28. See Pierre Lévy, *Cyberculture* (Minneapolis: University of Minnesota Press, 1997), 30.
29. On the virtual number-work relationship Quéau writes: "What is the substance of the virtual work? The model and the image, the intelligible and the sensible, each contribute for their part to the essence of the work, to the fundamental idea. But it is numbers that substantially unite the intelligible representation (the model) and the sensible representation (the image). It is therefore numbers that form the "substance" of the virtual work. It must be pointed out that the term "substance" is here used in a solely metaphorical sense. However, since numbers are what provide for the unity of the work, such metaphor takes on an analogical sense.... It evokes the relationship between the multiplicity of the potential or virtual manifestations of the work, and the formal unity that so constitutes it as *a work,*" Philippe Quéau, *Le virtuel. Vertus et vertige* (Seyssel: Champ Vallon/INA, 1993), 136.

30. For a synthetic exposition of the main theoretical approaches to the "cyborg," see Roberto Marchesini, *Post-human. Verso nuovi modelli di esistenza* (Turin: Bollati Boringhieri, 2002), 227–38.
31. The most famous case is that of Stelarc, whose hyperprosthetic body can be now manipulated by users on the Internet.
32. "The cyber body is not a subject, but an object . . . the cyber body becomes an extensive system—not merely in order to sustain itself, but in order to improve its operations and to launch alternative intelligent systems. The physical bodies inserted in the technology of the virtual reality are translated internally into spectral entities capable of representation. . . . The nature of both, body and image, is significantly altered. The images are not more illusory: when becoming interactive they are operational agents and effectual implementations within the software system and its transmission." See Stelarc, "From Psycho-Body to Cyber-Systems: Images as Post-Human Entities," in *Virtual Futures. Cyberotics, Technology, and Post-Human Pragmatism,* ed. J. Bradhurst Dixon and E. J. Cassidy (New York: Routledge, 1998), 121–22.
33. A reconstruction of this can be found in Jay David Bolter and Richard Grusin, *Remediation. Understanding New Media* (Cambridge: MIT Press, 2000). To my knowledge, the most recent and relevant text on this argument is Mark B. N. Hansen, *New Philosophy for New Media* (Cambridge: MIT Press, 2004), which also contains, starting from a consideration of the question of the corporeality of the user, an interesting analysis of artworks, especially those by Jeffrey Shaw. On the general question of the technologicization of the body, to which we shall return shortly, there are interesting texts in *Il corpo tecnologico,* ed. P. L. Capucci (Bologna: Baskerville, 1994).
34. Consequently, the study of the body and sensibility at the physiological level is essential for the construction of virtual environments; there is much to gain in this direction from a classic in the literature on virtual reality, such as *Silicon Mirage* by Aukstakalnis and Blatner. On techniques in particular, see Grigore C. Burdea, *Force and Touch Feedback for Virtual Reality* (New York: John Wiley and Sons, 1996).
35. Anne Balsamo, *Technologies of the Gendered Body: Reading Cyborg Women* (Durham: Duke University Press, 1996), 124–25.

36. "[The virtual self] does not learn by scientific study in a subject-object relationship, but by 'immersion,' which produces empathy and identification. The technique of visual immersion distinguishes virtual reality from the classic transparent medium, linear-perspective painting," Bolter and Grusin, *Remediation,* 251. This obviously does not mean that the difference between the virtual and the real is lost.
37. The possibility of making someone else's point of view one's own does not seem to me to be a contradiction.
38. Bolter's and Grusin's references to William James's concept of the self are, for our purposes, interesting and profound. See Bolter and Grusin, *Remediation,* 267–68.
39. Quéau , *Le virtuel,* 19.
40. Ibid., 18. I am not agreeing however with Quéau 's theory of intermediary entities and I elaborate the question in my own way.
41. Wassily Kandinsky, *Point and Line to Plane* (New York: Dover, 1979), 17.
42. See Michel Henry, *Seeing the Invisible: On Kandinsky* (New York: Continuum, 2009).
43. Consider the experiments conducted on virtual acrophobia at the Georgia Institute of Technology: users suffering from acrophobia in these virtual environments, environments that are not particularly convincing from the perceptual point of view, demonstrate the same symptoms that they would in "real" environments. The virtual environment allows patients to test and control their reactions in the absence of danger.
44. Bolter and Grusin, *Remediation,* 195.
45. A reconstruction of this can be found in Achille Varzi, *Parole, oggetti, eventi* (Rome: Carocci, 2001), 39–62.
46. But shadows and light rays can be screened out and so are not quite as penetrating as angels and ghosts.
47. Deutsch, *The Fabric of Reality,* 120.
48. "The particular character of objects, as compared to that of ideas or imaginings, is such that they cannot be amended by a simple act of volition, and thus belong to the outside world. . . . This feature concerns above all objects of perception (I cannot turn the apple that I have before me into a pear)." Maurizio Ferraris, "Problemi di ontologia applicata: la proprietà delle idee," in *Significato*

e ontologia, ed. C. Bianchi, and A. Bottani (Milan: Franco Angeli, 2003), 107.

49. And of course one knows how to individuate and signify a "simple volition."
50. We can ask ourselves if dreams are bodies, and, therefore, whether they are internal or external. We in fact know that the dream cannot be amended by a simple act of will, so if it is a body, it should be "external," and if it is not a body, it would remain to be clarified just what a body is, considering that a dream appears to be perceptually indistinguishable, physiologically and physically, from an environment made up of bodies. I shall return later to the discussion of dreams.
51. See Roberto Diodato, *Sub specie aeternitatis. Luoghi dell'ontologia spinoziana* (Milan: Cusl, 1990), 158–74.
52. An ontology of this type, however, has the need to make rigorous the concept of the instant in such a way that it would not depend on the concepts of time and duration, and this implies both a philosophy of the physics of time and a metaphysics of time. We will return to this last point later.

CHAPTER 2. *MY* BODY IN THE VIRTUAL ENVIRONMENT

1. For an account of this it is sufficient to skim through the indexes of the MIT review, *Presence: Teleoperators and Virtual Environments.* For an extremely effective updated summary of the diverse positions, see Antonella Carassa, Francesca Morganti, and Maurizio Tirassa, "Movement, Action, and Situation: Presence in Virtual Environments," in the Proceedings of the 7th Annual International Workshop on Presence (Presence 2004, Valencia Spain, 13–15 October, 2004), ed. M. Alcañiz Raya and B. Reyz Solaz (Valencia: Editorial Universidad Politecnica de Valencia, 2004), 7–12.
2. This may produce some confusion: "The work done so far is fragmentary and unsystematic, in part because scholars interested in the question of presence come from different disciplinary fields, (to include communication sciences, psychology, cognitive science, computer science, engineering, philosophy, and the whole scope of the arts)"; see Matthew Lombard and Theresa Ditton, "At the

Heart of It All: The Concept of Presence," *Journal of Computer-mediated Communication* 2 (1997): 5. The long essay provides a very extensive bibliography (http://www.ascusc.org/jcmc/vol3/issue2/lombard.html).
3. Lombard-Ditton, 15–17.
4. Wijnand Ijsselstein and Giuseppe Riva, "Being There: The Experience of Presence in Mediated Environments," in *Being There: Concepts, Effects, and Measurement of User Presence in Synthetic Environments,* ed. G. Riva, F. Davide, and W. Ijsselstein, (Amsterdam: Ios Press, 2003), 5.
5. Elena Pasquinelli, "Oggetti e presenza in realtà virtuale," *Sistemi intelligenti* XV, no. 3: 479.
6. Ibid.: 480.
7. Ibid.
8. See P. Zahoric, and R. L. Jenison, "Presence as Being-in-the-World," *Presence: Teleoperators and Virtual Environments* 7 (1998): 78–89.
9. See Giuseppe Mantovani and Giuseppe Riva,"'Real' Presence: How Different Ontologies Generate Different Criteria for Presence, Telepresence, and Virtual Presence," *Presence: Teleoperators and Virtual Environments* 8, no. 5 (1999): 540–50.
10. See Carassa, Morganti, and Tirassa, *Movement, Action, Situation: Presence in Virtual Environments.* The authors demonstrate very well the complexity that must be taken into account in the evaluation of "presence" in virtual environments due to the nonreducibility of the levels of interaction (situation, action, perception); "The classic dichotomy between the external world objectively given, and the internal world that faithfully reflects it (as any discrepancies would be misrepresentation), is unable to capture the interactive nature of human action. The meaning of any entity lies in the affordances that are permitted of agents, and these affordances are not properties of objects in the world, but properties of the interaction between agent and object"; see ibid., 5.
11. Appropriately, the authors emphasize the function and weight of memory: "The affordances depend on the activities in which the agent is involved at the time. Such activities result from the agent's preceding history, which goes on to constitute both memory and the processes of recognition and reconceptualization that render it

immediately useful in the current action," ibid., 6. I shall return to the question of memory shortly.
12. Edmund Husserl, *Formal and Transcendental Logic* (The Hague: Martinus Nijhoff, 1969), 247.
13. Vincenzo Costa makes a good summary of the question in his *L'estetica trascendentale e fenomenologica. Sensibilità e razionalità nella filosofia di Edmund Husserl* (Milan: Vita e Pensiero, 1999), 29–37.
14. Ibid., 30–31.
15. Edmund Husserl, *Cartesian Meditations* (Dordrecht: Kluwer, 1991), 76.
16. Jacques Derrida, *The Problem of Genesis in Husserl's Philosophy* (Chicago: University of Chicago Press, 2003), 153.
17. Valeria Ghiron, *La teoria dell'immaginazione di Edmund Husserl. Fantasia e coscienza figurale nella "fenomenologia descrittiva"* (Venice: Marsilio, 2001), 178.
18. This is described well by Elio Franzini: "Imagination is variation, which allows the passage from the variety of contingent vital forms, with their games, to the stable essence that renders possible the identity of the object with itself, which is determined by "changing" the look around it: it is therefore through it that we can express *the possible sense of our common life-world*," Elio Franzini, *Verità dell'immagine* (Milan: Il Castoro, 2004), 116. For a comprehensive look at the question of the imagination and in particular its different meanings in Husserl, see Carmelo Calì, "Husserl e l'immagine," *Aesthetica Preprint: Supplementa* 10 (2002).
19. Ms. E III 9/49a, cited in Vincenzo Costa, *L'estetica trascendentale e fenomenologica*, 35.
20. See Costa, *L'estetica trascendentale e fenomenologica,* part III.
21. Donna Haraway, "A Manifesto for Cyborgs" in *The Postmodern Turn: New Perspectives on Social Theory* (Cambridge: Cambridge University Press, 1994), 83.
22. Mariella Combi, *Corpo e tecnologie* (Rome: Meltemi, 2000), 119.
23. See Gilles Deleuze and Félix Guattari, *Capitalisme et schizophrénie. Mille plateaux* (Paris: Minuit, 1980), 636–37. For the English translation, see Gilles Deleuze and Félix Guattari, *A Thousand Plateaus: Capitalism and Schizophrenia* (New York: Continuum, 1980).

24. G. Boccia Artieri, *Lo sguardo virtuale*, 231.
25. Ibid.
26. On the problem of translating the term *Leib*, see Nathalie Depraz, "Postface: la traduction de Leib, une crux phaenomenologica," in Edmund Husserl, *Sur l'intersubjectivité* (Paris: PUF, 2001), 391–392.
27. Jean-Luc Nancy, *Corpus* (New York: Fordham University Press, 2008), 17.
28. Ibid.
29. Ibid., 121.
30. Ibid., 63.
31. I am thinking, obviously, of a reinterpretation of the living body from the point of view of the world's flesh. I believe, in short, that Merleau-Ponty has already moved on to Nancy's *Corpus*.
32. Maurice Merleau-Ponty, *Phenomenology of Perception* (London: Routledge, 1989), 146.
33. Ibid., 92.
34. Ibid., 84.
35. Ibid., 109.
36. Ibid., 137.
37. Ibid., 143.
38. Ibid., 404.
39. Kant would not agree with us (see for example his *Dreams of a Visionary Explained by Dreams of Metaphysics*). On this issue, see the beautiful chapter by Elio Franzini, "La vita è sogno," in *Fenomenologia dell'invisibile* (Milan: Cortina, 2001), 43–58.
40. Gottfried W. Leibniz, *New Essays on Human Understanding* (Cambridge: Cambridge University Press, 1996), 375.
41. See *Dreaming as Cognition*, ed. C. Cavallero and D. Foulkes, (London: Harvester Wheatsheaf, 1993).
42. Antonella Carassa and Maurizio Tirassa, "Essere nel mondo, essere nel sogno," in *Il sogno in psicoterapia cognitiva*, ed. G. Rezzonico and D. Liccione, (Turin: Bollati Boringhieri, 2004), 19.
43. Ibid.
44. See William Farthing, *The Psychology of Consciousness* (Englewood Cliffs: Prentice-Hall, 1992).
45. This follows Vittorio Guidano, *Il sé nel suo divenire* (Turin: Bollati Boringhieri, 1991).

46. See especially Francisco J. Varela, Evan Thompson, and Eleanor Rosch, *The Embodied Mind. Cognitive Science and Human Experience* (Cambridge: MIT Press, 1992), esp. 147–84.
47. On the basis of, for example, Andy Clark, *Being There: Putting Brain, Body, and World Together Again* (Cambridge: MIT Press, 1998); and Giuseppe Mantovani, *L'elefante invisibile* (Florence: Giunti, 1998).
48. Carassa andTirassa, "Essere nel mondo, essere nel sogno."
49. Ibid.
50. Ibid., 20.
51. "For how does one know that the thoughts that come to us in dreams are any more false than the others, given that they are often no less vivid and explicit? And even if the best minds study this as much as they please, I do not believe they can give any reason sufficient to remove this doubt, unless they presuppose the existence of God"; see René Descartes, *Discourse on Method* (Indianapolis: Hackett, 1998), 21.
52. "We are always immersed in the world, because this is the nature of our mind; but whereas in movies or daydreaming the world also includes fantastic stories without exhausting itself in them, in dreams world and story simply coincide without the slightest distance"; see Carassa andTirassa, "Essere nel mondo, essere nel sogno," 48.
53. Ibid., 21.
54. Ibid.
55. Gerald E. Edelman, *Bright Air, Brilliant Fire: On the Matter of the Mind* (New York: Perseus, 1992), 203–204.
56. Carassa and Tirassa, "Essere nel mondo, essere nel sogno," 9.
57. This is the "clamping" of which Glenberg speaks; see Arthur M. Glenberg, "What Memory is for," in *Behavioral and Brain Sciences* 20 (1997): 1–55.
58. See the discussion of this possibility in Maurizio Ferraris, *La conoscenza del mondo esterno* (Milan: Bompiani, 2001), 130–34.
59. See Massimo Negrotti, *Theory of the Artificial: Virtual Replications and the Revenge of Reality* (Exter: Intellect Books, 1999), 87–92 in particular for the classification of the virtual; see ibid., 137–50 on virtual reality.
60. Georges Simondon, *Du mode d'existence des object techniques* (Paris: Aubier Montaigne, 1969), 124. It would certainly be important,

for our theme, to rethink with care Simondon's theory of individuation, and more generally to rethink the meaning of technique and the relationship between art and technique. See on this point Pietro Montani, "Arte e tecnica. Una questione riaperta," in *Analysis* 3 (2004).

NOTES TO CHAPTER 3. FORMS OF EXPRESSION

1. This is confirmed by the contributions collected in Andrea Borsari, ed., *Politiche della mimesis. Antropologia, rappresentazione, performatività* (Milan: Mimesis, 2003). For a very accurate reconstruction of the constellation of meanings now covered by the concept, see the essay by Borsari, "'Mimesis,' le peripezie di una famiglia concettuale," 7–26 and 281–306. For a theoretical history of the concept, see Arne Melberg, *Theories of Mimesis* (Cambridge: Cambridge University Press, 1995). For mimesis as an aesthetic category, see Stephen Halliwell, *The Aesthetics of Mimesis* (Princeton: Princeton University Press, 2002).
2. See René Girard, *Things Hidden Since the Foundation of the World* (New York: Continuum, 2003), 283–99.
3. Gunter Gebauer and Christoph Wulf, "Mimesis," in *Encyclopedia of Aesthetics*, vol. 3, ed. M. Kelly (Oxford: Oxford University Press, 1998), 238.
4. But on this point Gebauer and Wulf have a different view: for them the advent of virtual worlds leads us to define mimesis as a thing of the past "when the gap between the mimetic world and the empirical world is reduced, empirical reality loses its autonomy against the world interpreted as mimetic. There is no reality beyond the world interpreted and cited; mimesis is no longer another world. It has become a self-illustration, a self-presentation"; see Gunter Gebauer and Christoph Wulf, *Mimesis. Kultur-Kunst-Gesellschaft* (Reinbeck: Rowohlt, 1992), 437.
5. Hans-Georg Gadamer, *Truth and Method* (New York: Continuum, 2002), 132.
6. Ibid., 133.
7. Ibid., 131.
8. Ibid., 132.
9. Ibid., 133.

10. Ibid., 135.
11. Ibid.
12. Ibid.
13. Ibid.
14. Ibid., 136. [Trans. Note: The translation has been modified to follow the Italian].
15. "It seems established that *bilidi* in Old High German always has the primary meaning of 'power,'" ibid., 169.
16. Ibid., 142.
17. On *Osmosis* see the accurate analysis by Oliver Grau, *Virtual Art. From Illusion to Immersion* (Cambridge: MIT Press, 2003), 193–202; see also Heim, *Virtual Realism,* 162–67. Davies's subsequent work *Ephemera* (1998) is also important, in that it allows one, among other things, to "penetrate" into the body and its organs.
18. Pierre Lévy, *Cyberculture,* 21–22.
19. Andrea Balzola and Anna Monteverdi, *Le arti multimediali digitali* (Milan: Garzanti, 2004), 472.
20. As stated on their website: www.studioazzurro.com.
21. This aspect of the digital image is emphasized and explored by Jean-Clet Martin, *Essai sur la construction du monde* (Paris: Editions Kimé, 1997).
22. Nelson Goodman, *Languages of Art* (Indianapolis: Hackett, 1976), 38.
23. I have elaborated the sense of Goodman's extraordinary philosophical work in my "Costruzionismo prospettico: Nelson Goodman," *Rivista di filosofia* 2 (2000): 51–60.
24. Goodman, *Languages of Art,* 230–31.
25. Ibid., 229–30.
26. Ibid., 231.
27. Ibid., 170.
28. Ibid., 171.
29. Ibid., 230.
30. Ibid., 231.
31. Ibid., 7–8.
32. Nelson Goodman, *The Structure of Appearance* (Dordrecht: Kluwer, 1977), xlix.
33. Ibid., 100.
34. Mario Perniola, *La società dei simulacri* (Bologna: Cappelli, 1983), 20. This text constitutes the second part of Mario Perniola, *Ritual*

Thinking, trans. Massimo Verdicchio (Amherst, NY: Humanity Books, 2001).
35. As observed by Mario Perniola. See the chapter, "Icon, Visions, Simulacra," in Perniola, *Ritual Thinking*, 158–72.
36. Perniola, *La società dei simulacri*, 121–22; trans. modified.
37. Ibid., 122.
38. Interesting is the way in which Perniola develops this thesis by making reference to Ignatius of Loyola and Bellarmine, and focusing on a relevant aspect of Jesuit humanism.
39. Perniola, *La società dei simulacri*, 127–28.
40. On this point, Débray writes: "with the 'infographic' image, simulation abolishes the simulacrum, thus removing the immemorial curse that combines image and imitation"; see Régis Débray, *Vita e morte dell'immagine* (Milan: il Castoro, 1999), 231, but see also 231–37.
41. Jean Baudrillard, "Simulacra and Simulations," in *Selected Writings* (Stanford: Stanford University Press, 2002), 173.
42. See Jean Baudrillard, *Symbolic Exchange and Death* (London: Sage, 1993).
43. Ibid., 133.
44. Jean Baudrillard, *Seduction* (New York: Macmillan, 1990), 69.
45. Jean Baudrillard, *The Perfect Crime* (London: Verso, 1996), 27. The "Postfazione" to the Italian translation by G. Piana well describes the evolution in Baudrillard's thought.
46. Ibid., 29–30.
47. Ibid., 110.
48. Ibid., 88.
49. Paolo Vidali, "Esperienze e comunicazione nei nuovi media," in G. Bettetini and F. Colombo, *Le nuove tecnologie della comuniczione* (Milan: Bompiani, 1998), 306.
50. Fausto Colombo, *Ombre sintetiche* (Naples: Liguori, 1995), 56–57.

CHAPTER 4. TOWARD THE IMAGE

1. Jean-Jacques Wunenburger, *Filosofia delle immagini* (Turin: Einaudi, 1999), 137.
2. On this dream see my article, "Narrazione e teodicea. Nota su un racconto di Leibniz," in *Vigilantia silentiosa et eloquens. Studi*

di filosofia in onore di Leonardo Verga, ed. F. De Capitani (Milan: Franco Angeli, 2001), 63–76.
3. Gilles Deleuze, *The Fold: Leibniz and the Baroque* (London: Continuum, 2006), 119.
4. This appears in a note in margin to Gottfried Wilhelm Leibniz, "*Specimen inventorum de admirandis naturae generalis arcanis.*"
5. G. W. Leibniz, "Monadology" in *Philosophical Essays* (Indianapolis: Hackett, 1989), §57, 220.
6. Ibid., §56.
7. See Donald Rutherford, "Phenomenalism and the Reality of Body in Leibniz's Later Philosophy," *Studia Leibnitiana* 22 (1990): 11–28, which offers an account of the debate on this issue.
8. Deleuze, *The Fold: Leibniz and the Baroque*, 127.
9. Now, to make this transition it would be necessary to investigate just what "bond" is, a strange word glorified in Giordano Bruno and that plagued the later Leibniz, leading him to construct an ambiguous position. In fact, the problem of "bond" matters for aesthetics in general, as it involves issues of perception, corporeality, space, time, in short, of the external and therefore of representation, of relation and therefore of harmony, of the finite and of the infinite. It is not a question that in its overall scope can now be addressed. On this argument see the classic studies by Maurice Blondel, *De vinculo substantiali et de substantia composita apud Luibnitium* (Paris: Alcan, 1893), and *Une énigme historique. Le "Vinculum substantiale" d'apres Leibniz et l'ébauche d'un réalisme supérieur* (Paris: Beauchesne, 1930); A. Boehm, *Le "Vinculum substantiale" chez Leibniz. Ses origines historiques* (Paris: Vrin, 1938). For an introduction to the question, see Alessandro Delcò, *Le metamorfosi della sostanza in Leibniz. Momenti di una teoria* (Milan: Franco Angeli, 1994), 99–111.
10. Precisely in the theoretical framework of the Trinitarian processions; I follow Question 35 of the first part of Thomas of Aquinas's *Summa Theologica,* entitled, "Of Image," in which he shows that Image is the "proper name" of the Son.
11. For an introduction to the various aspects of the relations between time and the virtual, see Derrick de Kerckhove, "La conquista del tempo," in *La conquista del tempo* (Rome: Editori Riuniti, 2003), 7–26.
12. Jean-Paul Sartre, *Immagine e coscienza. Psicologia fenomenologica*

dell'immaginazione (Turin: Einaudi, 1980).
13. Wunenburger, *Filosofia delle immagini*, 253.
14. Jean-Paul Sartre, *Imagination: A Psychological Critique* (Ann Arbor: University of Michigan Press, 1962), 2.
15. Ibid., 134.
16. Sartre, *Immagine e coscienza*, 13–14.
17. Ibid., 15.
18. Ibid., 16.
19. Ibid., 17.
20. "In one of the two cases the chair is met by consciousness, in the other it is not. But the chair is not in consciousness even as an image. This is not a simulacrum of a chair penetrated suddenly into consciousness and having only an 'extrinsic' relation to the existing chair, but a certain kind of consciousness, that is, a synthetic organization referring directly to the existing chair, and whose innermost essence consists precisely in this manner (and sometimes other manners) of reference to the existing chair," ibid., 17–18.
21. Ibid., 22.
22. Ibid., 21.
23. Ibid., 24.
24. Ibid., 30.
25. Ibid.
26. In fact, for Sartre, "the imagination is not an empirical power superimposed onto consciousness; it is consciousness as a whole, as it realizes its freedom. Each concrete and real state of consciousness in the world is fraught with imagery, insofar as it always presents itself as an overcoming of the real"; ibid., 286–87.
27. Sartre also realizes that dream analysis could call into question the difference between perceptual image and mental image, and attempts to defend such a distinction, in my view without success; see *Immagine e coscienza*, 248–73.
28. See my article, "Per un'estetica dell'incarnazione," *Hermeneutica* (2003): 27–39, at least for the critiques made by Henry and Deleuze.
29. For an excellent summary of the question, see Mauro Carbone, "Carne," *aut aut* 304 (2001): 99–119.
30. At least as configured in the Husserl of *Ideen I*. It is from quite another Husserl that Merleau-Ponty draws his philosophy of the

flesh of the world capable of thinking about excess and externality; it is from a 1934 manuscript designated with the title, *Umsturz der kopernikanischen Lehre*, which Merleau-Ponty was able to read in 1939 at the Husserl archives in Louvain. On the influence of this manuscript on Merleau-Ponty, see G. D. Neri, "Terra e cielo in un manoscritto husserliano del 1934," *aut aut* 245 (1991): in particular 38–44.

31. Maurice Merleau-Ponty, *The Visible and the Invisible* (Evanston: Northwestern University Press, 1968), 147. This is obviously a development of Husserl's example in *Ideen II*, chapter 36.
32. "The meditation must relearn a way of being whose idea has become lost for[the Copernican man], that is, the being of 'soil' (*Boden*), and especially that of the Earth"; Merleau-Ponty, "Husserl ai limiti della fenomenologia (1959–60)," in *Linguaggio Storia Natura. Corsi al Collège de France, 1952–1961,* ed. Mauro Carbone (Milan: Bompiani, 1995), 122.
33. "There is a reciprocal insertion and intertwining of one in the other. Or rather, if, as once again we must, we eschew the thinking by planes and perspectives, there are two circles, or two vortexes, or two spheres, concentric when I live naïvely, and as soon as I question myself, the one slightly decentered with respect to the other"; see Merleau-Ponty, *The Visible and the Invisible,* 138.
34. Edmund Husserl, *Formal and Transcendental Logic* (The Hague: Martinus Nijhoff, 1977), 292.
35. Merleau-Ponty, *The Visible and the Invisible,* 139.
36. This is contrary to what is claimed by Gilles Deleuze and Fèlix Guattari, *Che cos'è la filosofia?* (Turin: Einaudi, 1996), 184–85.
37. Merleau-Ponty, *The Visible and the Invisible,* 250.
38. I note only that the shift from "world" to "life" that Michel Henry considers essential is simply a shift of emphasis, that is, that life ("*pathos,* the grip without deviation and without the look of a suffering or rejoicing, which, as phenomenological material, is pure affection, pure impressionality, the radically immanent self-affection being none other than our flesh") is actually the flesh of the world, and indeed the ontological expansion of life in the world can afford a better grasp of the original receptive dimension, which Henry justly believes to be essential and that effectively allows him to emphasize the elusiveness of flesh to the grip of reason;

see Michel Henry, *Incarnazione. Una filosofia della carne* (Turin: Sei, 2001).

CHAPTER 5. METAPHORS OF THE VIRTUAL

1. G. Boccia Artieri, *Lo sguardo virtuale* (Milan: Franco Angeli, 1998), 241.
2. Tim McFadden, "Notes on the Structure of Cyberspace and the Ballistic Actors Model," in *Cyberspace: First Steps* (Cambridge: MIT Press, 1991), 341.
3. Lévy, *Cyberculture,* 74.
4. Michael Benedikt, "Cyberspace: Some Proposals," in *Cyberspace: First Steps,* 131.
5. Marcos Novak, "Liquid Architecture in Cyberspace," in *Cyberspace: First Steps,* 234.
6. See Elisabetta Locatelli, "*Spazio e tempo nei mondi virtuali,*" dissertation in philosophy discussed at the Università Cattolica del Sacro Cuore during the academic year 2002–03.
7. Mariella Combi, *Corpo e tecnologie. Simbolismi, rappresentazioni e immaginari* (Rome: Meltemi, 2000), 122.
8. Pierre Lévy, *Collective Intelligence: Mankind's Emerging World in Cyberspace* (Cambridge: Perseus, 1997).
9. Peter Russell, *The Global Brain Awakens* (Saline: McNaughton and Gunn, 1995).
10. See Roberto Diodato and P. Ferri, "Dall'individuo virtuale alla communità personale," in *Individuo e rapporto comunitario,* ed. R. Cotteri (Merano: Accademia di studi italo-tedeschi, 1996), 511–30; and Roberto Diodato and P. Ferri, "Il concetto di comunità virtuale," in *L'Europa multiculturale* (Merano: Accademia di studi italo-tedeschi, 1998), 336–43. On the concept of virtual community, see P. Carbone and P. Ferri, eds., *La comunità virtuale* (Milan: Mimesis, 1999), and the second chapter of Paolo Ferri, *La rivoluzione digitale* (Milan: Mimesis, 1999), 45–114.
11. These are investigated by Giorgio Agamben, *The Coming Community* (Minneapolis: University of Minnesota Press, 1990).
12. Jean-Luc Nancy, *The Inoperative Community* (Minneapolis: University of Minnesota Press, 1991).

13. Jean-Luc Nancy, "Being-in-Common," in *Community at Loose Ends* (Minneapolis: University of Minnesota Press, 1991), 4.
14. Ibid.
15. Ibid.
16. Nancy connects in an interesting way the theme of "co-appearing" to that of "temporality," referring to a problem that we will have to examine, in Jean-Luc Nancy, *Being Singular Plural* (Stanford: Stanford University Press, 2000).
17. Pierre Lévy, *Collective Intelligence* (Cambridge: Perseus Books, 1997), 168.
18. An example might be the phenomenon of blogs, and thus the renewed communicative potentialities of autobiographical writing.
19. Nancy, *Community at Loose Ends*, 8. Here, Nancy is backed up by a complex and glorious phenomenological, personalist, and even existentialist tradition that is nowadays quite mistreated.
20. McFadden, "Notes on the Structure of Cyberspace and the Ballistic Actors Model", 341.
21. This feature is highlighted by Silvano Tagliagambe, *Il sogno di Dostoevskij* (Milan: Cortina, 2002), 265.
22. Quéau, *Le virtuel*, 13–14.
23. Ibid., 14.
24. Novak, "Liquid Architecture in Cyberspace," in Benedikt, *Cyberspace*, 244.
25. Ibid.
26. Tagliagambe, *Il sogno di Dostoevskij*, 269.
27. Tomás Maldonado deals with virtual space as perceptual space in *Critica della ragione informatica* (Milan: Feltrinelli, 1999), 156–57.
28. See James J. Gibson, *The Ecological Approach to Visual Perception* (Hillsdale: Lawrence Erlbaum Associate, 1986), ch. 5. Meo rightly observes: "Gibson focuses more on relations than on things. It is precisely relational constancy that enables figural recognition despite the variation of the same forms"; see Oscar Meo, *Mondi possibili. Un'indagine sulla costruzione percettiva dell'oggetto estetico* (Genoa: Il Melangolo, 2002), 148. It is a matter of relations among objects and not of objects that are relations; that is, a structurally different field than the one we are investigating comes to be thus constituted.
29. I am obviously taking advantage of Arnheim's remarkable proposal for what it can offer to my purposes; I am not, however, interested

in discussing the key concepts of his theory, for example, the coherence of the notion of meaningfulness and the like, nor am I interested in the relation, as articulated by Arnheim, between psychology and art (including the problem of what he means by "art", etc.).

30. Rudolph Arnheim, *Art and Visual Peception: A Psychology of the Creative Eye* (Berkeley: University of California Press, 1974), 437–38.
31. Ibid., 42–43.
32. Ibid., 44.
33. Ibid., 45.
34. Ibid., 47.
35. Ibid., 48.
36. Ibid., 49.
37. Ibid.
38. Ibid., 98.
39. See Lucia Pizzo Russo, *Le arti e la psicologia* (Milan: Il Castoro, 2004), 176–77.
40. Ibid., 101.
41. Ibid., 181.
42. On this distinction, see Elio Franzini, "La rivelazione della realtà: espressione e simbolo in R. Arnheim," in *Rudolf Arnheim: arte e percezione visiva*, ed. L. Pizzo Russo, Aesthetica Preprint: Supplementa 14 (2005).
43. For de Kerckhove, who coined the singular expression, "volcanic arts," "art comes from technology. It is the opposing force that balances the disruptive effects of new technologies in culture. Art is the metaphorical aspect of the same technology that it uses and criticizes," in *La pelle della cultura. Un'indagine sulla nuova realtà elettronica*, ed. Ch. Dewdney (Genoa: Costa and Nolan, 1996), 174. On de Kerckhove's aesthetics, see Lorella Scacco, *Estetica mediale* (Milan: Guerini, 2004), 27–39.
44. For a description of this, see de Mérédieu, *Arts et nouvelles technologies*, 158.
45. Emanuele Quinz, "Interface world. Mutazioni della scena: dal testo all'ambiente," in *La scena digitale*, ed. A. Menicacci and E. Quinz (Venice: Marsilio, 2001), 328–29.
46. Some theorizations and applications in the field of theater try to transition from an interface-environment to a world-environment, for example, the experimentation, *Intelligent Stage,* by Robb Lowell

at The Institute for Studies in the Arts (Arizona). See A. M. Monteverdi, "Per un teatro tecnologico," in *Le arti multimediali digitali*, 247–348.
47. Edmond Couchot, *La technologie dans l'art. De la photographie à la réalité virtuelle* (Nîmes: J. Chambon, 1998), 144.
48. See Roberto Diodato, "Spinoza, Leibniz: alternative per l'estetica," in *Il paesaggio dell'estetica. Teorie e percorsi* (Turin: Trauben, 1997), 195–203.
49. On Spinoza one must of course defer to Gilles Deleuze, *Expressionism in Philosophy: Spinoza* (Brooklyn: Zone Books, 1990); and on Leibniz we now have available the remarkable work by Antonio Somaini, *Espressione, proiezione, rispecchiamento. La teoria leibniziana della rappresentazione*, a doctoral thesis in philosophy (2001–02) that also provides an account of the literature on this topic.
50. See Jean-Jacques Wunenburger, *Filosofia delle immagini* (Turin: Einaudi, 1999), 164–168.
51. L. W Stern, "Il tempo di presenza psichico (1897)," in *La percezione degli eventi. Ricerche di psicologia sperimentale*, ed. G. Vicario and E. Zambianchi (Milan: Guerini, 1998), 31.
52. For an approach to the philosophical problems of time from the point of view of physics, see M. Pauri, "La descrizione fisica del mondo e la questione del divenire temporale," in *Filosofia della fisica*, ed. G. Boniolo (Milan: Bruno Mondadori, 1997), 245–333.
53. On this problem, see G. Vicario, "Tempo della fisica e tempo della psicologia," in G. Vicario and E. Zambianchi, *La percezione degli eventi. Ricerche di psicologia sperimentale* (Milan: Guerini, 1998), 69–99. Also of interest on this theme is M. Dorato, *Futuro aperto e libertà. Un'introduzione alla filosofia del tempo* (Rome-Bari: Laterza, 1997), esp. 248–65.
54. On this point relative to artistic production, see the interview of Christine Buci-Glucksmann by Edmond Chouchot, "*Arts et temps virtuels*," in *L'art à l'époque du virtuel*, ed. Christine Buci-Glucksmann, (Paris: L'Harmattan, 2003), 95–101.
55. On this see Vicario, *Introduzione a La percezione degli eventi*, 12–14.
56. On this note, Heidegger maintains that Hegel's treatment of time depends essentially on that of Aristotle; see Martin Heidegger, *Being and Time*, trans. Macquarrie and Robinson (New York: Harper and Row, 1962), 500, note XXX.

57. Jacques Derrida, "*Ousia* and *grammé*", in *Margins of Philosophy* (Chicago: University of Chicago Press, 1982), 34.
58. Ibid., 55.
59. Ibid.
60. Ibid., 56.
61. Ibid., 59.
62. Ibid., 60.
63. Ibid.
64. Ibid., 62.
65. Ibid., 61–62.
66. Ibid, 63.
67. Derrida, whom I want to remember as one of the greatest philosophers of the twentieth century, attempted to construct a quasi-transcendental philosophy, that is, a philosophy that displays how philosophy's necessity of defining the transcendental conditions for the thinkability of experience leads necessarily to establishing the impossibility of such conditions, or rather, to the fact that such conditions are impossible possibilities. Consequently, the philosophical work is structurally tied to an aporetic situation. The exposition of such a condition takes on many names in Derrida's texts (gift, forgiveness, specter, Messiah, and so on).
68. One could show, however, that as thought of becoming, the potentiality-actuality relation expresses an analogy with the relation between act of being and essence, which are really distinct co-principles of the entity, the former being the ground of positivity, and the latter being the ground of the limitation of such positivity; in this way, the very possibility of the entity's nonexistence is built into the essence of the entity itself.

CHAPTER 6. THE CONCEPT OF THE VIRTUAL

1. Pierre Lévy, *Becoming the Virtual* (New York: Basic Books, 1998), 23.
2. Ibid., 24–25.
3. Ibid., 24.
4. Ibid., 171.
5. See the first chapter of the present work.
6. Lévy, *Becoming the Virtual,* 172.

7. Ibid., 173.
8. Ibid.
9. This could be understood only within a scholastic formalism, which we are not going to analyze here, which thinks the entity as *id quod habet vel potest habere esse* [that which has and can have being].
10. Lévy, *Becoming the Virtual*, 178.
11. Ibid.
12. Ibid.
13. With the caveat that Whitehead did not accept Einstein's theory of space as non-uniform. See Alfred N. Whitehead, *The Concept of Nature* (London: Cambridge University Press, 1920).
14. Gilles Deleuze, *Difference and Repetition* (New York: Continuum, 2004), 263.
15. Gilles Deleuze, *Proust and Signs* (Minneapolis: University of Minnesota Press, 2000), 63.
16. This is Deleuze's way of accepting Bergson's legacy. An attentive rereading of Gilles Deleuze, "Memory as Visual Coexistence," in *Bergsonism* (New York: Zone Books, 2006), 51–72, is essential. Attention on this issue is drawn by Pier Aldo Rovatti in his "Introduction" to the Italian translation of Deleuze's *Bergsonism*.
17. Deleuze, *Bergsonism*, 97.
18. Ibid., 105.
19. See, for example, Gilles Deleuze, *A Thousand Plateaus: Capitalism and Schizophrenia* (New York: Continuum, 1988), 109.
20. Zourabichvili has pointed out that Deleuze does not hypothesize a passage "from the virtual to the actual, from time to the body, as from a transcendental principle to its consequence, as if he pursued the metaphysical task of deducing existence. . . . We cannot leave the virtual aside, even and especially in a philosophy of immanence: . . . "pluralism = monism," univocality. . . . The virtual is by no means a second world, does not exist outside bodies, although it does not resemble their actuality. . . . The abstraction begins only when begins to separate the body from the virtual implied in it, when one takes into account only the disembodied appearance of pure actuality (representation)." See François Zourabichvili, *Deleuze. Una filosofia dell'evento* (Verona: Ombre corte, 1998), 89–90.
21. Gilles Deleuze, "L'attuale e il virtuale," in Gilles Deleuze and Claire Parnet, *Conversazioni* (Verona: Ombre corte, 1998), 158–61.

22. Deleuze, *Difference and Repetition,* 261.
23. Gilles Deleuze, *Cinema 2: The Time Image* (London: Continuum, 1989), 80.
24. Deleuze, *Conversazioni,* 160.
25. Ibid., 161.
26. For a very interesting development of Deleuzean time-image in the direction of the virtual, see Jean-Louis Weissberg, "Commentaires sur l'image actée, à partir de L'image-temps de Gilles Deleuze," in *Présence à distance* (Paris: L'Harmattan, 1999), ch. VI, 207–38.
27. Deleuze, *Cinema 2: The Time-Image,* 69.
28. Ibid.
29. Ibid., 70.
30. Ibid., 79.
31. Ibid., 81.
32. Ibid., 121.
33. Gilles Deleuze and Félix Guattari, *What is Philosophy?* (New York: Columbia University Press, 1994), 118.
34. Ibid., 156.
35. Interesting in this regard is what Jean-Clet Martin writes connecting the problem of virtual reality to that "Bathos" "not only obscure, but undefined and nothing," which Étienne Souriau theorizes in his thinking about reality. See Jean-Clet Martin, "Réalités virtuelles," in *L'art à l'époque du virtuel,* 204.
36. The figure of chaos, in this regard and in relation to the question of potentiality, was taken up in a profound way by Giordano Bruno. See Roberto Diodato, "L'ombra di Bruno," in *La pluralità estetica,* ed. G. Marchianò (Turin: Trauben, 2001), 63–77.

CHAPTER 7. THE VIRTUAL ACTOR-SPECTATOR

1. Quéau, *Le virtuel,* 20.
2. Through the idea of an intermediary entity, Quéau tries to interpret the relation between potentiality and virtuality, principles interwoven in virtual bodies, environments-bodies, or "worlds," which "are virtual because of the virtual presence of the models within the images that show them, and potential in relation to the generative power of the models themselves" (*Le virtuel,* 27), and are therefore actualized (or realized, as Quéau does not distinguish between the two operations) in interaction. Quéau also tries to

think of movement as intermediary between potentiality and actuality (see on this point Philippe Quéau, *Metaxu. Théorie de l'art intermédiaire* (Champ Vallon-INA, 1989), 96–97).

3. From this concept, Quéau traces the idea of an "intermediary art," focusing *inter alia* on the interesting idea that computers "facilitate the design of programs that are restructured in view of their results"; see Quéau, *Metaxu,* 332. For a development of the idea of intermediary art, see Jacques Lafon, *Pour une esthétique de l'image de synthèse. La trace de l'ange* (Paris: Harmattan, 1999).

4. Quéau, *Le virtuel,* 14.

5. For an introduction to the idea of the "active spectator," see Andrew Darley, *Visual Digital Culture. Surface Play and Spectacle in New Media Genres* (London: Routledge, 2000), 173–78.

6. Bolter and Grusin, *Remediation,* 165–67.

7. See Étienne Souriau, "La structure de l'univers filmique et le vocabulaire de la filmologie," in *L'univers filmique,* ed. É. Souriau (Paris: Flammarion, 1953).

8. For the following distinctions regarding the forms of cinematic perspective, see Francesco Casetti, *Dentro lo sguardo. Il film e il suo spettatore* (Milan: Bompiani, 2001), in particular, chs. 2 and 3. See also Francesco Casetti and Federico Di Chio, *Analisi del film* (Milan: Bompiani, 1999), 243–48.

9. "Shooting camera" is, in Italian, "*macchina da presa.*" "*Presa,*" meaning, "hold," "grip," "capture," connotes a sense of grasping that is lost in the English translation [Trans.].

10. Edgar Morin, *Il cinema o l'uomo immaginario* (Milan: Feltrinelli, 1982), especially the preface.

11. Carmagnola reflects on these themes, and combines the virtual and cinema in virtue of the notion of hypertext; see Fulvio Carmagnola, *Plot, il tempo del raccontare* (Rome: Meltemi, 2004), 116–62.

12. See André Bazin, *Che cosa è il cinema* (Milan: Garzanti, 1986).

13. See Sergei Eisenstein, *Il montaggio (1923–40),* ed. P. Montani (Venice: Marsilio, 1986).

CHAPTER 8. FOR AN AESTHETICS OF THE HYPERTEXT

1. For several definitions see Domenico Fiormonte, *Scrittura e filologia nell'era digitale* (Turin: Bollati Boringhieri, 2003), 80–106.

2. George P. Landow, *Hypertext: The Convergence of Contemporary Critical Theory and Technology* (Baltimore: Johns Hopkins University Press, 1997), 3–4.
3. Ibid., 313–14, note 1. The reference is to the essay by Dorothy Lee, "Lineal and Nonlineal Codifications of Reality," in *Symbolic Anthropology: A Reader in the Study of Symbols and Meanings*, ed. J. L. Dolgin, D. S. Kemnitzer, and D. M. Schneider (New York: Columbia University Press, 1977), 151–64.
4. For example, consider Góngora's extreme, almost absurd work on language undertaken for the purpose of bending it towards nonlinearity; on this point see Roberto Diodato, *Vermeer, Góngora, Spinoza. L'estetica come scienza intuitiva* (Milan: Bruno Mondadori, 1997), 203–64.
5. On the relation between literary criticism and hypertextuality, see Alberto Cadioli, *Il critico navigante. Saggio sull'ipertesto e la critica letteraria* (Milan: Marietti, 1998).
6. See Alexander G. Baumgarten, *Reflections on Poetry* (Los Angeles: University of California Press, 1954).
7. See Fausto Colombo and Ruggero Eugeni, *Il testo visibile* (Florence: La Nuova Italia Scientifica, 1996), 197.
8. Gianfranco Bettetini, Barbara Gasparini, and Nicoletta Vittadini. *Gli spazi dell'ipertesto* (Milan: Bompiani, 1999), 58.
9. I take the term in Deleuze's sense. See Gilles Delezue, *Francis Bacon: The Logic of Sensation* (New York: Continuum, 2005). On the virtual environment as haptic space, see Mark B. N. Hansen, *New Philosophy for New Media*, 110–21.
10. See Maurice Merleau-Ponty, "Eye and Mind," in *Basic Writings* (New York: Routledge, 2004), 312.

Bibliography

Agamben, Giorgio. *The Coming Community*. Minneapolis: University of Minnesota Press, 1990.
Alliez, Eric. "Pour une phénoménology réelle des images virtuelles." *Chimeres* (Hiver 1996): 123–33.
Arnheim, Rudolph. *Art and Visual Perception: A Psychology of the Creative Eye*. Berkeley: University of California Press, 1994.
Artieri, Giovanni Boccia. *Lo sguardo virtuale*. Milan: Franco Angeli, 1998.
Balsamo, Anne. *Technologies of the Gendered Body: Reading Cyborg Women*. Durham: Duke University Press, 1996.
Balzola, Andrea, and Anna Monteverdi. *Le arti multimediali digitali*. Milan: Garzanti, 2004.
Baudrillard, Jean. *Seduction*. New York: MacMillan, 1990.
———. "Simulacra and Simulations." In *Selected Writings*. Stanford: Stanford University Press, 2002.
———. *Symbolic Exchange and Death*. London: Sage, 1993.
———. *The Perfect Crime*. London: Verso, 1996.
Bazin, André. *Che cosa è il cinema*. Milan: Garzanti, 1986.
Benedikt, Michael. "Cyberspace: Some Proposals." In *Cyberspace: First Steps*. Cambridge: MIT Press, 1991.
Bettetini, Gianfranco, and Fausto Colombo, *Le nuove tecnologie della comunicazione*. Milan: Bompiani, 1998.
Bettetini, Gianfranco, Barbara Gasparini, and Nicoletta Vittadini. *Gli spazi dell'ipertesto*. Milan: Bompiani, 1999.
Bolter, Jay David, and Richard Grusin. *Remediation. Understanding New Media*. Cambridge: MIT Press, 2000.

Borsari, Andrea, ed. *Politiche della mimesis. Antropologia, rappresentazione, performatività.* Milan: Mimesis, 2003.
Burdea, Grigore C. *Force and Touch Feedback for Virtual Reality.* New York: Wiley, 1996.
Cadioli, Alberto. *Il critico navigante. Saggio sull'ipertesto e la critica letteraria.* Milan: Marietti, 1998.
Cadoz, Claude. *Les réalités vituelles.* Paris: Flammarion, 1994.
Calì, Carmelo. "Husserl e l'immagine." *Aesthetica Preprint: Supplementa* 10 (2002).
Capucci, Pierluigi. *Realtà del viruale. Rappresentazioni tecnologiche, comunicazione, arte.* Bologna: Clueb, 1993.
―――, ed. *Il corpo tecnologico. L'influenza delle tecnologie sul corpo e sulle sue facoltà.* Bologna: Baskerville, 1994.
Carassa, Antonella, and Maurizio Tirassa. "Essere nel mondo, essere nel sogno." In *Il sogno in psicoterapia cognitiva,* ed. G. Rezzonico and D. Liccione. Turin: Bollati Boringhieri, 2004.
―――, Francesca Morganti, and Maurizio Tirassa. "Movement, Action, and Situation: Presence in Virtual Environments." In *Proceedings of the 7th Annual International Workshop on Presence,* ed. M. Raya and Reyz Solaz, 7–12. Valencia: Editorial Universidad Politécnica de Valenica, 2004.
Carbone, Mauro. "Carne." *Aut aut* 304 (2001): 99–119.
Carbone, Paola, and Paolo Ferri, eds. *Le comunità virtuali.* Milan: Mimesis, 1999.
Carmagnola, Fulvio. *Plot, il tempo del raccontare.* Rome: Meltemi, 2004.
Caronia Antonio. *Il corpo virtuale. Dal corpo robotizzato al corpo disseminato nelle reti.* Padua: Muzzio, 1996.
Casetti, Francesco. *Dentro lo sguardo. Il film e il suo spettatore.* Milan: Bompiani, 2001.
―――, and Federico Di Chio. *Analisi del film.* Milan: Bompiani, 1999.
Cavallero, Corrado, and David Foulkes, eds. *Dreaming as Cognition.* London: Harvester Wheatsheaf, 1993.
Chateau, Dominique, and Bernard Darras, eds. *Arts et multimedia. L'oeuvre d'art et sa reproduction à l'ère des medias interactifs.* Paris: Publications de la Sorbonne, 1999.

Clark, Andy. *Being There: Putting Brain, Body, and World Together Again.* Cambridge: MIT Press, 1998.
Clenberg, A. M. "What Memory Is For." *Behavioral and Brain Sciences* 20 (1997): 1–55.
Colombo, Fausto. *Ombre sintetiche. Saggio di una teoria dell'immagine elettronica.* Naples: Liguori, 1995.
———, and Ruggero Eugeni, *Il testo visibile.* Florence: La Nuova Italia Scientifica, 1996.
Combi, Mariella. *Corpo e tecnologie. Rappresentazioni e immaginari.* Rome: Meltemi, 2000.
Costa, Mario. *Il sublime tecnologico. Piccolo trattato di estetica della tecnologia.* Rome: Castelvecchi, 1998.
Costa, Vincenzo. *L'estetica trascendentale e fenomenologica. Sensibilità e razionalità nella filosofia di Edmund Husserl.* Milan: Vita e Pensiero, 1999.
Couchot, Edmond. *La technologie dans l'art. De la photographie à la réalité virtuelle.* Nîmes: J. Chambon, 1998.
———, and Norbert Hillaire. *L'art numérique.* Paris: Flammarion, 2003.
Danelli, Diana. "Per una scultura digitale a bassa densità." In *Nel foco che li affina. Quattro studi per Francesco Piselli*, 23–44. Milan: Prometheus, 2000.
D'Alessandro, Paolo. *Critica della ragione telematica. Il pensiero in rete e le reti del pensiero.* Milan: LED, 2002.
Darley, Andrew. *Visual Digital Culture. Surface Play and Spectacle in New Media Genres.* London: Routledge, 2000.
Débray, Régis. *Vita e morte dell'immagine.* Milan: il Castoro, 1999.
De Kerckhove, Derrick. *The Skin of Culture: Investigating the New Electronic Reality.* Toronto: Somerville House, 1995.
———. "La Conquista Del Tempo." In *La Conquista Del Tempo*, 7–26. Rome: Editori Riuniti, 2003.
De Méredieu, Florence. *Arts et nouvelles technologies. Art vidéo, Art numérique.* Paris: Larousse, 2003.
Delcò, Alessandro. *Le metamorfosi della sostanza in Leibniz. Momenti di una teoria.* Milan: Franco Angeli, 1994.
Deleuze, Gilles. *Bergsonism.* New York: Zone, 2006.
———. *Cinema 2: The Time Image.* London: Continuum, 1989.

———. *Difference and Repetition*. New York: Continuum, 2004.
———. "L'attuale e il virtuale." Gilles Deleuze and Claire Parnet. In *Conversazioni*. Verona: Ombre Corte, 1998.
———. *Proust and Signs*. Minneapolis: University of Minnesota Press, 2000.
———. *The Fold: Leibniz and the Baroque*. London: Continuum, 2006.
———, and Félix Guattari. *A Thousand Plateaus: Capitalism and Schizophrenia*. New York: Continuum, 1980.
———. *What Is Philosophy?* New York: Columbia University Press, 1994.
Deloche Bernard. *Le musée virtuel. Vers une éthique des nouvelles images*. Paris: PUF, 2001.
Depraz, Nathalie. "Postface: La traduction de *Leib*, une crux phaenomenologica." In *Edmund Husserl, Sur L'intersubjectivité*, 391–92. Paris: PUF, 2001.
Derrida, Jacques. "*Ousia* and *Grammé*." In *Margins of Philosophy*. Chicago: University of Chicago Press, 1982.
———. *The Problem of Genesis in Husserl's Philosophy*. Chicago: University of Chicago Press, 2003.
Descartes, René. *Discourse on Method*. Indianapolis: Hackett, 1998.
Deutsch, David. *The Fabric of Reality: The Science of Parallel Universes—and Its Implications*. New York: Penguin, 1997.
Diodato, Roberto. "Costruzionismo prospettico: Nelson Goodman." *Rivista di filosofia* 2 (2000): 51–60.
———. "Narrazione e teodicea. Nota su un racconto di Leibniz." In *Vigilantia silentiosa et eloquens. Studi Di Filosofia in Onore Di Leonardo Verga*, ed. F. De Capitani, 63–76. Milan: Franco Angeli, 2001.
———. *Sub specie aeternitatis. Luoghi dell'ontologia spinoziana*. Milan: Cusl, 1990.
Druckrey, Timothy, and Ars Electronica, eds. *Ars Electronica: Facing the Future*. Cambridge: MIT Press, 1999.
Duguet, Anne-Marie. *Déjouer l'image. Créations électroniques et numériques*. Nîmes: Jacqueline Chambon, 2002.
Edelman, Gerald E. *Bright Air, Brilliant Fire: On the Matter of the Mind*. New York: Perseus, 1992.
Eisenstein, Sergei. *Il montaggio (1923–40)*. Ed. P. Montani. Venice: Marsilio, 1986.
Farthing, William. *The Psychology of Consciousness*. Englewood Cliffs: Prentice-Hall, 1992.

Ferraris, Maurizio. *La conoscenza del mondo esterno*. Milan: Bompiani, 2001.

———. "Problemi di ontologia applicata: La proprietà delle idee." In *Significato e ontologia*, ed. C. Bianchi and A. Bottani. Milan: Franco Angeli, 2003.

Ferri, Paolo. *La rivoluzione digitale*. Milan: Mimesis, 1999.

Fiormonte, Domenico. *Scrittura e filologia nell'era digitale*. Turin: Bollati Boringhieri, 2003.

Franzini, Elio. "La vita è sogno." In *Fenomenologia dell'invisibile*, 43–58. Milan: Cortina, 2001.

———. *Verità dell'immagine*. Milan: Il Castoro, 2004.

Gadamer, Hans-Georg. *Truth and Method*. New York: Continuum, 2002.

Gebauer, Gunter, and Christoph Wulf. *Mimesis. Kultur-Kunst-Gesellschaft*. Reinbeck: Rowohlt, 1992.

Ghiron, Valeria. *La teoria dell'immaginazione di Edmund Husserl. Fantasia e coscienza figurale nella fenomenologia descrittiva*. Venice: Marsilio, 2001.

Gibson, James J. *The Ecological Approach to Visual Perception*. Hillsdale: Lawrence Erlbaum, 1986.

Gilead, Amihud. "How Many Pure Possibilities Are There?" *Metaphysica. International Journal for Ontology and Metaphysics* 2 (2004): 89–90.

Girard, René. *Things Hidden Since the Foundation of the World*. New York: Continuum, 2003.

Glenberg, Arthur M. "What Memory Is For." *Behavioral and Brain Sciences* 20 (1997): 1–55.

Goodman, Nelson. *Languages of Art*. Indianapolis: Hackett, 1976.

———. *The Structure of Appearance*. Dordrecht: Kluwer, 1977.

Grau, Oliver. *Virtual Art: From Illusion to Immersion*. Cambridge: MIT Press, 2003.

Guidano, Vittorio. *Il sé nel suo divenire*. Turin: Bollati Boringhieri, 2004.

Halliwell, Stephen. *The Aesthetics of Mimesis*. Princeton: Princeton University Press, 2002.

Hansen, Mark B. N. *New Philosophy for New Media*. Cambridge: MIT Press, 2004.

Haraway, Donna. "A Manifesto for Cyborgs." In *The Postmodern Turn: New Perspectives on Social Theory*. Cambridge: Cambridge University Press, 1994.

———. *Simians, Cyborgs, and Women: The Reinvention of Nature.* London: Free Association Books, 1991.
Heidegger, Martin. *Being and Time.* Trans. John MacQuarrie and Edward Robinson. New York: Harper and Row, 1962.
Heim, Michael. *The Metaphysics of Virtual Reality.* Oxford: Oxford University Press, 1993.
———. *Virtual Realism.* New York: Oxford University Press, 1998.
Henry, Michel. *Seeing the Invisible: On Kandinsky.* New York: Continuum, 2009.
Hillis, Ken. *Digital Sensation. Space, Identity, and Embodiment in Virtual Reality.* Minneapolis: University of Minnesota Press, 1999.
Husserl, Edmund. *Cartesian Meditations.* Dordrecht: Kluwer, 1991.
———. *Formal and Transcendental Logic.* The Hague: Martinus Nijhoff, 1969.
Ijsselstein, Wijnand, and Giuseppe Riva. "Being There: The Experience of Presence in Mediated Environments." In *Being There: Concepts, Effects, and Measurement of User Presence in Synthetic Environments,* ed. G. Riva, W. Ijsselstein, and F. Davide. Amsterdam: Ios, 2003.
Kandinsky, Wassily. *Point and Line to Plane.* New York: Dover, 1979.
Koepsell, David. *The Ontology of Cyberspace. Philosophy, Law, and the Future of Intellectual Property.* Chicago: Open Court, 2000.
Lafon, Jacques. *Pour une esthétique de l'image de synthèse. La trace de l'ange.* Paris: Harmattan, 1999.
Landow, George P. *Hypertext: The Convergence of Contemporary Critical Theory and Technology.* Baltimore: Johns Hopkins University Press, 1997.
Leibniz, Gottfried W. *The Monadology.* London: Routledge, 2002.
———. *New Essays on Human Understanding.* Cambridge: University of Cambridge, 1996.
———. *Philosophical Essays.* Indianapolis: Hackett, 1989.
Lévy, Pierre. *Collective Intelligence: Mankind's Emerging World in Cyberspace.* Cambridge: Perseus, 1997.
———. *Becoming the Virtual.* New York: Basic, 1998.
———. *Cyberculture.* Minneapolis: University of Minnesota Press, 1997.
Lombard, Matthew, and Theresa Ditton, "At the Heart of It All: The Concept of Presence." *Journal of Computer-mediated Communication,* 2 (1997).

Maldonado, Tomás. *Critica della ragione informatica*. Milan: Feltrinelli, 1999.
Mantovani, Giuseppe. *L'elefante invisibile*. Florence: Giunti, 1998.
———, and Giuseppe Riva. "'Real' Presence: How Different Ontologies Generate Different Criteria for Presence, Telepresence, and Virtual Presence." *Presence: Teleoperators and Virtual Environments* 5 (1999): 540–50.
Marchesini, Roberto. *Post-human. Verso nuovi modelli di esistenza*. Turin: Bollati Boringhieri, 2002.
Martin, Jean-Clet. *Essai sur la construction du monde*. Paris: Editions Kimé, 1997.
Massumi, Brian. *Parables of the Virtual: Movement, Affect, Sensation*. Durham: Duke University Press, 2002.
McFadden, Tim. "Notes on the Structure of Cyberspace and the Ballistic Actors Model." In *Cyberspace: First Steps,* 245–375. Cambridge: MIT Press, 1991.
Melberg, Arne. *Theories of Mimesis*. Cambridge: Cambridge University Press, 1995.
Meo, Oscar. *Mondi possibili. Un'indagine sulla costruzione percettiva dell'oggetto estetico*. Genoa: Il Melangolo, 2002.
Merleau-Ponty, Maurice. "Eye and Mind." In *The Merleau-Ponty Reader,* 351–78. Evanston: Northwestern University Press, 2007.
———. "Husserl ai limiti della fenomenologia." In *Linguaggio Storia Natura. Corsi al Collège De France, 1952–1961,* ed. Mauro Carbone. Milan: Bompiani, 1995.
———. *Phenomenology of Perception*. New York: Routledge, 1989.
———. *The Visible and the Invisible*. Evanston: Northwestern University Press, 1968.
Montani, Pietro. "Arte e tecnica. Una questione riaperta." *Analysis* 3 (2004).
Morin, Edgar. *Il cinema o l'uomo immaginario*. Milan: Feltrinelli, 1982.
Nancy, Jean-Luc. *Corpus*. New York: Fordham University Press, 2008.
———. *Being Singular Plural*. Stanford: Stanford University Press, 2000.
———. "Being-in-Common." *Community at Loose Ends*. Minneapolis: University of Minnesota Press, 1991.
———. *The Inoperative Community*. Minneapolis: University of Minnesota Press, 1991.

Negrotti, Massimo. *Theory of the Artificial: Virtual Replications and the Revenge of Reality.* Exeter: Intellect Book, 1999.

Novak, Marcos. "Liquid Architecture in Cyberspace." In *Cyberspace: First Steps,* ed. Michael Benedikt, 233–65. Cambridge: MIT Press, 1991.

Pasquinelli, Elena. "Oggetti e presenza in realtà virtuale." *Sistemi intelligenti* 3 (2003): 475–91.

Paul, Christiane. *Digital Art.* London: Thames and Hudson, 2003.

Perniola, Mario. *La società dei simulacri.* Bologna: Cappelli, 1983.

Pizzo Russo, Lucia. *Le arti e la psicologia.* Milan: Il Castoro, 2004.

Porchet, Michel. *La production industrielle de l'image. Critique de l'image de synthese.* Paris-Budapest-Turin: L'Harmattan, 2002.

Quéau, Philippe. *Eloge de la simulation.* Seyssel: Champ Vallon-INA, 1986.

———. *Le virtuel. Vertus et vertige.* Seyssel: Champ Vallon-INA, 1993.

———. "Les vois virtuelles du savoir." In *Costruzione e appropriazione del sapere nei nuovi scenari tecnologici,* ed. A. P. Gambardella. Naples: CUEN, 1998.

———. *Metaxu. Théorie de l'art intermédiaire.* Champ Vallon, 1989.

Quinz, Emanuele. "Interface-World. Mutazioni della scena: Dal testo all'ambiente." In *La scena digitale,* ed. A. Menicacci and E. Quinz, 317–34. Venice: Marsilio, 2001.

Rheingold, Howard. *Virtual Reality.* New York: Simon and Schuster, 1991.

Rivoltella, Pier Cesare. "La multimedialità." In *Tecniche e significati. Linee per una nuova didattica formativa,* ed. C. Seurati, 219–58. Milan: Vita e Pensiero, 2000.

Russell, Peter. *The Global Brain Awakens.* Saline: McNaughton and Gunn, 1995.

Rutherford, Donald. "Phenomenalism and the Reality of Body in Leibniz's Later Philosophy." *Studia Leibnitiana* 22 (1990): 11–28.

Sapin, T. K., I. S. Pandzic, N. Magnenat-Thalmann, and D. Thalmann. *Avatars in Networked Virtual Environments.* Chichester-New York: Wiley, 1999.

Sartre, Jean-Paul. *Imagination: A Psychological Critique.* Paris: Presses Universitaires de France, 1962.

———. *Immagine e coscienza. Psicologia fenomenologica dell'immaginazione.* Turin: Einaudi, 1980.

Scacco, Lorella. *Estetica mediale.* Milan: Guerini e Associati, 2004.

Schroeder, Ralph, ed. *The Social Life of Avatars. Presence and Interaction in Shared Virtual Environments.* London: Springer-Verlag, 2002.

Sherman, William R., and Alan B. Craig. *Understanding Virtual Reality. Interface, Application, and Design.* Amsterdam: Morgan Kaufmann, 2003.

Simondon, Georges. *Mode d'existence des object techniques.* Paris: Aubier Montaigne, 1969.

Souriau, Étienne. "La structure de l'univers filmique et le vocabulaire de la filmologie." In *L'univers filmique,* ed. É. Souriau. Paris: Flammarion, 1953.

Stelarc. "From Psycho-Body to Cyber-Systems: Images as Post-Human Entities." In *Virtual Futures. Cyberotics, Technology, and Post-Human Pragmatism,* ed. J. B. Dixon and E. J. Cassidy, 116–23. New York: Routledge, 1998.

Stern, L.W. "Il tempo di presenza psichico." In *La percezione degli eventi. Ricerche di psicologia sperimentale,* ed. G. Vicario and E. Zambianchi. Milan: Guerini, 1998.

Steuer, J. "Definire la realtà virtuale: Le dimensioni che determinano la telepresenza." In *La communicazione virtuale: Dal computer alle reti telematiche: Nuove forme di interazione sociale,* ed. C. Galimberti and G. Riva, 55–78. Milan: Guerini and Associates, 1997.

Tagliagambe, Silvano. *Il sogno di Dostoevskij.* Milan: Cortina, 2002.

Taiuti, Lorenzo. *Corpi sognanti. L'arte nell'epoca delle tecnologie digitali.* Milan: Feltrinelli, 2001.

Tirassa, Maurizio. "Essere nel mondo, essere nel sogno." In A. Carassa, *Il sogno in psicoterapia cognitiva,* ed. G. Rezzonico and D. Liccione. Turin: Bollati Boringhieri, 2004.

Varela, Francisco J., Evan Thompson, and Eleanor Rosch. *The Embodied Mind. Cognitive Science and Human Experience.* Cambridge: MIT Press, 1992.

Varzi, Achille. *Parole, oggetti, eventi.* Rome: Carocci, 2001.

Ventimiglia, Giovanni. "Ontologia ed etica del virtuale." *Teoria* 1 (2004): 119–47.

Vidali, Paolo. "Esperienze e comunicazione nei nuovi media." In *Le Nuove Tecnologie Della Comunicazione,* ed. G. Bettetini and F. Colombo. Milan: Bompiani, 1998.

Weissberg, Jean-Louis. "Il compatto reale/virtuale." In *La scena immateriale. Linguaggi elettronici e mondi virtuali,* ed. A. Ferraro and G. Montagano, 46–59. Milan: Cortina, 1998.

Whitehead, Alfred N. *The Concept of Nature*. London: Cambridge University Press, 1920.
Wilson, John R. "Towards Real Applications of Virtual Environments: Ergonomics Research and Development." In *Virtual Reality. Select Issues and Applications,* ed. H.M. Khalid, 9–27. London: ASEAN Academic, 2000.
Wulf, Christoph. "Mimesis." In G. Gebauer, *Encyclopedia of Aesthetics,* ed. M. Kelly. Vol. 3. Oxford: Oxford University Press, 1998.
Wunenburger, Jean-Jacques. *Filosofia delle immagini*. Turin: Einaudi, 1999.
Zahoric, P., and R. L. Jenison. "Presence as Being-in-the-World." *Presence: Teleoperators and Virtual Environments* 7 (1998): 78–89.
Zourabichvili, François. *Deleuze. Una filosofia dell'evento*. Verona: Ombre corte, 1998.

Index

Actor, v, x, 23, 29, 47, 50, 75, 81, 101, 103, 105, 110, 137, 138, 153
Actuality, 10, 55, 88, 89, 91, 100, 141, 142, 144
Aisthesis, 7
Affective (affectivity), 9, 21, 25, 32, 102, 109
Agamben, Giorgio, 137, 147
Algorithm, 1, 6, 11, 13, 45, 82, 105
Alliez, Eric, 123, 147
Animal, vii, 40, 53
Aristotle, 84, 85, 140
Arnheim, Rudolph, 76–82, 138, 139, 147
Art, 37, 39, 40, 41, 45, 46, 48, 80, 81, 99, 101, 104, 105, 107, 109, 110, 116, 119, 120, 121, 126, 131, 139, 144
Artieri, Giovanni, 129, 137, 147
Artificial(ity), 9, 24, 25, 33, 43, 48, 51, 82, 104, 109, 110, 118, 130, 154
Artist, 7, 39
Author, 21, 39, 111, 112, 115, 116
Avatar, vii, viii, x, 2, 3, 26, 30–32, 60, 94, 120, 154, 155

Bakhtin, Mikhail, 111
Balsamo, Anne, 124, 147

Balzola, Andrea, 40, 132
Barthes, Roland, 102, 111
Baudrillard, Jean, 48–52, 133, 147
Becoming, 10, 11, 35, 54, 84, 87–89, 94, 100, 102, 141
Belief, 5, 15, 17, 104, 110, 122
Bergson, Henri, 84, 95, 99, 142, 149
Bettetini, Gianfranco, 133, 145, 147, 155
Bolter, Jay David, 102, 105, 124, 125, 144, 147
Brain, 11, 46, 71, 78, 116, 130, 137, 149, 151, 154
Burdea, Grigore, 124, 148

Cadioli, Alberto, 145, 148
Camera, 3, 8, 102–105, 144
Carassa, Antonella, 126, 127, 129, 130, 148, 155
Carmagnola, Fulvio, 144, 148
Cartesian, 29, 39, 128, 152. *See also* Descartes
Casetti, Francesco, 144, 148
Cinema(tic), 38, 98, 102–110, 143, 144, 147, 149, 153
Cognitivism, 27, 28
Coherence, 30, 32, 114, 139
Colombo, Fausto, 133, 145, 147, 149, 155

Combi, Mariella, 128, 137, 149
Communication, 13, 17, 38, 50, 51, 52, 66, 70, 71, 126, 127, 152
Community, 71–74, 137, 138, 147, 153
Conformity, 17, 54, 57
Consciousness, ix, 19, 25, 28–30, 50, 58–66, 80, 83, 129, 135, 150
Constructivism, 42, 77
Conventionalism, 42
Costa, Mario, 119, 149
Costa, Vincenzo, 128, 149
Couchot, Edmond, 121, 140, 149
Culture, 16, 101, 139, 144, 149
Cyberculture, 70, 123, 132, 137, 152
Cyberspace, 70, 74, 75, 117, 137, 138, 147, 152, 153, 154
Cyborg, 7, 25, 124, 128, 147, 151, 152

Danelli, Diana, 121, 149
Darley, Andrew, 144, 149
De Kerckhove, Derrick, 134, 139, 149
Death, 49, 133, 147
Debord, Guy, 50
Deleuze, Gilles, 55, 57, 91, 92, 95–99, 110, 123, 128, 134, 135, 136, 140, 142, 143, 145, 149, 150, 156
Depraz, Nathalie, 129, 150
Derrida, Jacques, 20, 84, 85, 111, 128, 141, 150
Descartes, René, 130, 150. *See also* Cartesian
Deutsch, David, 12, 122, 125, 150
Disembodiment, 8
Dream, viii, x, 13, 26–33, 54, 64, 98, 99, 109, 118, 126, 129, 130, 133, 135, 148

Eisenstein, Sergei, 108, 144, 150
Embodiment, 2, 8, 28, 92, 122, 152
Emotion(al), 3, 10, 21, 32, 70, 75, 101, 112
Epistemology, 46
Expression, v, 6, 26, 35, 39, 54, 55, 57, 58, 66, 67, 78, 80, 82, 131, 140

Feeling, viii, 7, 10, 15, 16, 20, 26, 29, 39–41, 67, 75, 104, 106
Ferraris, Maurizio, 125, 130, 151
Film, 8, 16, 62, 97, 102–105, 108, 110, 144, 148, 155
Flesh, 23, 61, 65–67, 129, 136
Foucault, Michel, 111
Franzini, Elio, 128, 129, 139, 151
Freedom, 5, 6, 20, 51, 80, 107, 113, 115, 116, 135
Future (the), 74, 80, 84, 85, 88, 96, 99, 124, 150, 152, 155

Gadamer, Hans-Georg, 37, 38, 131, 151
Gebauer, Gunter, 131, 151, 156
Gibson, James, 76, 110, 138, 151
Gilead, Amihud, 119, 151
Girard, René, 131, 151
Goodman, Nelson, 41, 42, 44–47, 132, 150, 151
Grau, Oliver, 4, 39, 121, 132, 151
Guattari, Félix, 128, 136, 143, 150

Haraway, Donna, 21, 151
Heidegger, Martin, 84, 87, 140, 152
Heim, Michael, 122, 123, 132, 152
Henry, Michel, 125, 135–137, 152
Hermeneutics, 78
Heterodirectionality, 31, 32, 110

Index

Historicity, 20, 21, 35, 47, 48
History, 12, 13, 17, 19, 20, 23, 66, 81, 82, 103, 127, 131
Hypermediacy, 102, 105
Hypertext, v, 70, 73, 107, 111–118, 144, 145, 152
Hypertextual(ity), 16, 115, 145
Husserl, Edmund, 19–21, 65, 66, 84, 128, 129, 135, 136, 149–153
Hypereal(ity), 48, 51

Icon, 1, 41, 44, 47, 48, 120, 133
Ijsselstein, Wijnand, 127, 152
Identification, 4, 10, 36, 77, 102, 104–107, 125
Illusion, viii, 5, 14–16, 36, 42, 50, 51, 98, 103–105, 121, 132, 151
Imagination, vii, 8, 13, 20–22, 39, 58, 61, 62, 64, 75, 80, 103, 128, 135, 154
Immanence, 61, 66, 73, 96, 99, 100, 142
Immediacy, 70, 102, 105
Immersion, x, 6, 8, 10, 15, 16, 30, 75, 103–106, 109, 110, 121, 122, 125, 132, 151
Immersive, 4, 8, 24, 29, 98, 101, 117
Immersiveness, 4, 8
Immersivity, 31, 74, 76, 105
Incoherence, 30, 31, 32
Intelligence, 71, 73, 105, 117, 118, 137, 138, 152
Intentional(ity), 19, 21, 22, 24, 25, 28–30, 60–65
Interactivity, 4, 6, 7, 11, 13, 16, 19, 22, 57, 76, 106, 113, 116, 130
Interface, 3, 75, 81, 82, 122, 139, 154, 155
Internet, 74, 105, 116, 117, 121, 124

James, William, 125

Kandinsky, Wassily, 4, 125, 152
Kant, Immanuel, 84, 109, 129

Landow, George, 111, 112, 145, 152
Law, 103, 113, 118, 152
Leibniz, Gottfried, 27, 54–57, 82, 115, 129, 133, 134, 140, 149, 150, 152, 154
Lévy, Pierre, 6, 39, 70, 73, 91–95, 123, 132, 137, 138, 141, 142, 152
Literary criticism, 145
Literature, 124, 140
Logic, 46, 57, 72, 88, 96, 107, 114–116, 128, 136, 145, 152
Lombard, Matthew, 126, 127, 152

Machine, 5, 6, 23–25, 33, 81, 82, 113
Mantovani, Giuseppe, 127, 130, 153
Martin, Jean-Clet, 132, 143, 153
Materiality, 4, 21, 40, 101, 109
Matrix, 2, 13, 55, 57, 120
McFadden, Tim, 69, 74, 137, 138, 153
Media, 47, 48, 51, 102, 124, 133, 144, 145, 147, 149, 151, 155
Memory, 2, 7, 9, 11–13, 27, 29–33, 60, 64, 75, 78, 78, 95–99, 127, 128, 130, 142, 144, 151
Merleau-Ponty, Maurice, x, 21, 23, 65, 66, 77, 118, 119, 120, 129, 135, 136, 145, 153
Metaphor(ical), v, 1, 4, 9, 56, 69, 70, 80, 88, 94, 107, 113–115, 117, 118, 123, 139
Metaphysics, 47, 49, 54, 86, 87, 94, 119, 123, 126, 129, 151, 152

Mimesis, 1, 17, 35–38, 41, 44, 49, 58, 82, 119, 131, 137, 148, 151, 153, 156
Modernity, 116
Monad, 54–57, 82, 94
Montage, 105, 108
Montani, Pietro, 120, 131, 144, 150, 153
Morin, Edgar, 104, 110, 144, 153
Multimedia(l), 2, 44, 102, 119, 132, 140, 147, 148
Multimediality, 4, 121,
Music(al), 42

Nancy, Jean-Luc, 24, 72, 129, 137, 138, 153
Narration, 107, 108, 112
Narrative, 27, 31, 32, 54, 104, 105, 107, 108, 110, 112
Networked Virtual Environment, 2, 120, 154
Noesis, 7, 64
Nominalism, 42, 71
Notation(al), 42–45
Novak, Marcos, 137, 138, 154

Objectivity, 17, 18, 26, 98, 102, 103
Ontological structure, 10, 17, 18, 20, 59, 99, 100
Ousia, 84, 97, 141, 150

Painting, 22, 37, 39, 43, 62, 101, 102, 125
Parousia, 84, 87
Past (the), 19, 46, 78, 84, 95, 96, 98, 99, 102, 131
Performance, 25, 27, 31, 45, 50, 104, 109
Perniola, Mario, 132, 133, 154
Phenomenology, 2, 8, 19, 20–22, 25, 64, 78, 120, 123, 129, 147, 153

Philosophy, vii, 18, 82, 91, 95, 99, 124, 126, 128, 134, 135, 140–143
Photography, 16, 38
Picture, 17, 22, 37, 38, 42–45, 50, 61, 62, 104
Pluralism, 46, 142
Poetry, 145
Post-human, 23, 124, 153, 155
Postmodern, 128, 151
Potentiality, x, 86–89, 93, 96, 100, 106, 141, 143, 144
Present (the), 31, 84, 86, 93, 95–99, 117
Prosthesis, x, 7, 8, 11, 13, 22–26, 35, 39, 45, 64
Psychology, 28, 60, 75, 82, 83, 107, 126, 129, 139, 147, 150

Quéau, Philippe, 8, 74, 101, 122, 123, 125, 138, 143, 144, 154

Realism, 42, 72, 122, 132, 134, 152
Reason, 14, 65, 78, 136
Relational, x, 1, 10, 35, 36, 41, 60, 63–65, 76, 82, 94, 100, 107, 113, 117, 120, 138
Relativism, 46, 47
Remediation, 102, 124, 125, 144, 147
Resemblance, 35, 36, 42–44, 46, 49, 53, 58, 61, 64, 95, 96, 102, 118
Reversibility, 65, 66, 94, 98, 118

Sartre, Jean-Paul, 21, 51, 58–64, 80, 135, 154
Science, 1, 35, 66, 99, 122, 126, 130, 149, 150, 151, 155
Scotus, Duns, 123
Sensation, x, 10, 16, 25, 29, 75, 82, 109, 122, 145, 152, 153
Sensibility, 114, 118, 124

Shape, 2, 4, 53, 60, 70, 76–81, 95, 99, 114
Simondon, Georges, 33, 130, 131, 155
Simulacrum, x, 1, 41, 44, 47–49, 51, 53, 62, 105, 108, 119, 133, 135
Simulation, 4–6, 8, 16, 22, 35, 42, 48, 49, 74, 77, 102, 105, 109, 121, 122, 133, 147, 154
Society, 50
Spectator, v, x, 29, 50, 75, 81, 101–110, 143, 144
Stelarc, 25, 124, 155
Subjectivity, 19–21, 50, 73, 94, 96, 116
Substance, 6, 10, 11, 40, 50, 55, 56, 70, 82, 88, 92–94, 1001, 113, 123
Symbol(ic), 17, 36, 42–47, 49, 53, 70, 80, 104, 114, 133, 145, 147
Symbolism, 80
Synaesthesia, 44

Tagliagambe, Silvano, 138, 155
Technology, 8, 13, 23, 35, 51, 111, 114, 117, 124, 125, 139, 145, 152, 155

Television, 16, 22, 62
Theater, 107, 109, 139
Tirassa, Maurizio, 126, 127, 129, 130, 148, 155
Transcendence, 66, 67
Transcendental, 19–22, 53, 54, 60, 65, 88, 93, 128, 136, 141, 142, 152
Translation, 1, 3, 28, 53, 75, 83, 93

Unilateralism, 28–30

Virtual field, 22, 24, 59, 60, 63,-65, 73, 76–78, 81
Virtual reality, vii, viii, x, 3–6, 10, 12, 21, 50, 51, 102, 108, 109, 117, 122–125, 130, 143, 148, 152, 154–156
Virtual space, 3, 8, 26, 69, 70, 74–77, 101, 138

Whitehead, Alfred, 93, 94, 142, 156
Wulf, Christoph, 131, 151, 156
Wunenburger, Jean-Jacques, 82, 133, 135, 140, 156

Zourabichvili, François, 142, 156

www.ingramcontent.com/pod-product-compliance
Lightning Source LLC
LaVergne TN
LVHW041206030526
837769LV00030B/349